W9-ASR-599

UNDERSTANDING
NEIL SIMON

Understanding Contemporary American Literature
Matthew J. Bruccoli, Series Editor

Volumes on

Edward Albee • Nicholson Baker • John Barth • Donald Barthelme
The Beats • The Black Mountain Poets • Robert Bly
Raymond Carver • Fred Chappel • Chicano Literature
Contemporary American Drama
Contemporary American Horror Fiction
Contemporary American Literary Theory
Contemporary American Science Fiction
James Dickey • E. L. Doctorow • John Gardner • George Garrett
John Hawkes • Joseph Heller • Lillian Hellman • John Irving
Randall Jarrell • William Kennedy • Jack Kerouac
Ursula K. Le Guin • Denise Levertov • Bernard Malamud
Bobbie Ann Mason • Jill McCorkle • Carson McCullers
W. S. Merwin • Arthur Miller • Toni Morrison's Fiction
Vladimir Nabokov • Gloria Naylor • Joyce Carol Oates
Tim O'Brien • Flannery O'Connor • Cynthia Ozick
Walker Percy • Katherine Anne Porter • Reynolds Price
Annie Proulx • Thomas Pynchon • Theodore Roethke
Philip Roth • Hubert Selby, Jr. • Mary Lee Settle
Neil Simon • Isaac Bashevis Singer • Jane Smiley
Gary Snyder • William Stafford • Anne Tyler
Kurt Vonnegut • Robert Penn Warren • James Welch
Eudora Welty • Tennessee Williams • August Wilson

UNDERSTANDING
NEIL SIMON

Susan Koprince

University of South Carolina Press

Published in Columbia, South Carolina, by the
University of South Carolina Press

Manufactured in the United States of America

06 05 04 03 02   5 4 3 2 1

Library of Congress Cataloging-in-Publication Data

Koprince, Susan Fehrenbacher, 1946–
    Understanding Neil Simon / Susan Koprince.
        p. cm. — (Understanding contemporary American literature)
Includes bibliographical references and index.
    ISBN 1-57003-426-5 (alk. paper)
    1. Simon, Neil—Criticism and interpretation. I. Title. II. Series.
PS3537.I663 Z74 2002
812'.54—dc21   2001006913

To my mother, Virginia Fehrenbacher,
and to the memory of my father, Don E. Fehrenbacher

CONTENTS

EDITOR'S PREFACE

The volumes of *Understanding Contemporary American Literature* have been planned as guides or companions for students as well as good nonacademic readers. The editor and publisher perceive a need for these volumes because much of the influential contemporary literature makes special demands. Uninitiated readers encounter difficulty in approaching works that depart from the traditional forms and techniques of prose and poetry. Literature relies on conventions, but the conventions keep evolving; new writers form their own conventions—which in time may become familiar. Put simply, *UCAL* provides instruction in how to read certain contemporary writers—identifying and explicating their material, themes, use of language, point of view, structures, symbolism, and responses to experience.

The word *understanding* in the titles was deliberately chosen. Many willing readers lack an adequate understanding of how contemporary literature works; that is, what the author is attempting to express and the means by which it is conveyed. Although the criticism and analysis in the series have been aimed at a level of general accessibility, these introductory volumes are meant to be applied in conjunction with the works they cover. They do not provide a substitute for the works and authors they introduce, but rather prepare the reader for more profitable literary experiences.

M. J. B.

PREFACE

Although Neil Simon has delighted audiences around the world for more than three decades, he has been largely ignored by literary scholars—partly because he appeals to the masses and partly because he writes comedy, a genre which some academics are reluctant to embrace. This book seeks to grant Simon the serious critical attention that he deserves. It offers an in-depth analysis of Simon's most notable plays, beginning with his first Broadway effort, *Come Blow Your Horn* (1961), and ending with one of his more recent comedies, *Laughter on the 23rd Floor* (1993). Because Simon is a remarkably prolific writer, I do not attempt to discuss all of his plays. Nor do I focus on Simon's musicals or on the many screenplays that he has written over the years. Instead, I provide a close reading of sixteen of Simon's comedies as well as an overview of his dramatic art. I try to demonstrate Simon's versatility, his craftsmanship, and his willingness to experiment with his comedic form. Most of all, I emphasize the serious nature of Simon's plays—not just the serious themes that he addresses, but also the Chekhovian blend of humor and pathos which pervades his drama.

I thank my daughter, Karen, for her generous assistance with the task of proofreading. I am also deeply grateful to my husband, Ralph, for his careful reading of my manuscript and his helpful suggestions for improvement.

CHAPTER ONE

UNDERSTANDING
NEIL SIMON

Understanding Neil Simon

Neil Simon once told an interviewer, "I think there is something special and unique in my story because it is kind of a Cinderella story."[1] Growing up in a poor Jewish American family in New York during the Great Depression, Simon eventually went on to become a celebrated writer of comedy and the most commercially successful playwright in the history of the American theater. Extremely prolific, Simon has written more than thirty play scripts as well as many television and radio scripts, screenplays, and a two-volume autobiography. During his career he has frequently had several plays running simultaneously on Broadway (at one point in 1966–67 he had four shows running), and his comedies have been highly popular with regional and amateur theater groups. Movie versions have been made of most of Simon's works, with the author writing virtually all of the screenplays himself. In 1986 *Time* estimated Simon's net worth at $30 million, and indeed, as Glenn Loney notes, "in terms of royalties and other income from his varied ventures on stage, in films, and on television," Simon may very well be considered the wealthiest playwright who ever lived.[2]

Marvin Neil Simon was born July 4, 1927, in the Bronx, New York, but later moved with his family to the Washington Heights section of Manhattan. His childhood was not a happy one, largely because of the tempestuous marriage of his parents, Irving and Mamie Simon. Simon's father, a garment salesman, deserted the family repeatedly during the playwright's youth, often staying away from home for months at a time. Occasionally Simon and his older brother, Danny, were forced to live with relatives, and Mamie Simon took in boarders to help support the family. "The horror of those years was that I didn't come from one broken home but five," remembers Simon. "It got so bad at one point that we took in a couple of butchers who paid their rent in lamb chops."[3] Simon sought escape from his traumatic home life in the movies, taking special pleasure in the comedies of Charlie Chaplin. At an early age he learned the importance of comedy as a defense mechanism: "I think part of what has made me a comedy writer is the blocking out of some of the really ugly, painful things in my childhood and covering it up with a humorous attitude. I knew that whenever things were so terrible at home, the best thing for me was to go to the movies—do something to laugh until I was able to forget what was hurting."[4]

When Simon was fifteen, he and Danny created a series of comedy sketches for the annual employees' show at Abraham and Straus, a department store for which Danny worked. After graduating at age sixteen from DeWitt Clinton High School in the Bronx, Simon entered an Army Air Force Reserve training program at New York University and in 1945 was sent to Lowry Field, Colorado, where he served as a corporal. It was during these years in the military that Simon began his writing career in earnest, covering a variety of sporting events for the Army Air Force and working as sports editor for the publication *Rev-Meter.*

After his discharge in 1946, Simon once again collaborated with his brother, Danny, landing a job with producer/writer Goodman Ace of CBS—a breakthrough opportunity that launched the brothers' careers as comedy writers. During the next decade Danny and "Doc" Simon (a nickname derived from Simon's childhood imitations of the family doctor) wrote comedy sketches for *The Robert*

UNDERSTANDING NEIL SIMON

Q. Lewis Show (radio) and for television comedians such as Phil Silvers, Jackie Gleason, and Sid Caesar. They also contributed material to two Broadway productions—*Catch a Star!* (1955) and *New Faces of 1956.* Eventually the Simon brothers went their separate ways. Danny moved to the West Coast to pursue a career in television directing, while Neil perfected his skills as a comedy writer. Earning Emmy awards in 1957 (for *The Sid Caesar Show*) and 1959 (for the *Sergeant Bilko* series), Simon continued working as a comedy writer for television until the production of his first Broadway play, *Come Blow Your Horn,* in 1961.

When *Barefoot in the Park* (1963) and *The Odd Couple* (1965) became long-running hits, Simon found himself a celebrity and the hottest new playwright on Broadway. Since that time he has proved his staying power with audiences, writing popular plays ranging from romantic comedy to farce to more serious comedy/drama. Simon has also successfully adapted other material for the stage— the musicals *Little Me* (1962) from the novel by Patrick Dennis, *Sweet Charity* (1966) from Federico Fellini's screenplay *Nights of Cabiria,* and *Promises, Promises* (1968) from the movie *The Apartment* by Billy Wilder and I. A. L. Diamond.

The quality of Simon's screenplays is uneven, perhaps because the author has never been as comfortable writing for Hollywood as for Broadway, where he exercises more control over his material. Nevertheless, Simon has created some effective adaptations of his own comedies—particularly *The Odd Couple* (Paramount, 1968), *The Sunshine Boys* (MGM, 1975), *California Suite* (Columbia, 1978), and *Biloxi Blues* (Universal, 1988). Simon's other screenplays range from disappointments such as *The Out-of-Towners* (Paramount,

1970) and *The Odd Couple II* (Paramount, 1998) to successful comedies such as *The Heartbreak Kid* (Twentieth Century Fox, 1972) and *The Goodbye Girl* (Warner Brothers, 1977). Inspired by a Bruce Jay Friedman story, *The Heartbreak Kid* describes how a man is smitten by one young woman while on his honeymoon with another; *The Goodbye Girl,* which starred Simon's second wife, Marsha Mason, depicts a romance between a single mother whose lover has deserted her and the struggling actor with whom she must share her New York apartment. Both movies reveal the pitfalls of romantic love, offering clever versions of one of Simon's most prevalent themes—the difficulty of maintaining long-term relationships.

Simon's many honors as a dramatist include the 1965 Tony Award for Best Playwright (*The Odd Couple*), a special Tony Award in 1975 for his overall contribution to the American theater, the New York Drama Critics Circle Award for *Brighton Beach Memoirs* (1983), the 1985 Tony Award for Best Play (*Biloxi Blues*), and the Best Play Tony Award as well as the Pulitzer Prize for *Lost in Yonkers* (1991). Broadway also paid tribute to him in 1983 by renaming the Alvin Theatre the Neil Simon Theatre.

The critical response to Simon over the last thirty-five years has been mixed—some reviewers admiring his comedic art and appreciating his blend of humor and pathos, others faulting him for his weak dramatic structure and his overreliance on gags and one-liners. Literary scholars have generally ignored Simon, regarding him as a commercially successful playwright rather than a serious dramatist. Since 1991, when Simon was awarded the Pulitzer Prize for drama, academics have shown an increased interest in Simon's work but not to the extent that he deserves. As Clive Barnes once wrote,

Simon, like his British counterpart, Noël Coward, "is destined to spend most of his career underestimated, rich and popular."[5]

According to Thomas Meehan, "an ability to write comedy is an innate talent that can't be taught, learned, bought, or even rationally explained. You either have it or you don't."[6] Neil Simon clearly possesses that comedic talent and has demonstrated it over the years in an impressive variety of plays, ranging from light romantic comedy and farce to more serious comedy/drama and dark comedy. Although Simon is willing to address almost any serious subject, he cannot envision writing a play that is completely without humor. "I see comedy—or humor . . . in almost everything that I've gone through in life," he says, "with the exception of my [first] wife's illness and death."[7] Simon generally works in the vein of domestic realism, but he occasionally experiments with nonrealistic technique—as in the Brighton Beach trilogy, in which the narrator, Eugene Jerome, breaks through the imaginary "fourth wall" on stage and speaks directly to the audience; or in the expressionistic *Jake's Women* (1992), in which the action takes place, to a large extent, in the mind of the protagonist.

Simon's plays invariably depict the plight of white middle-class Americans, most of whom are New Yorkers and many of whom are Jewish. As John Lahr has suggested, Simon's theater is aimed at "the silent majority"—those people who have a romantic craving for sex, adventure, and new experiences but who are helpless to change, wedded as they are to their bourgeois life.[8] Frustrated, edgy, and insecure, Simon's characters have special difficulty maintaining long-term relationships, whether it be within a marriage, a friendship, or a business partnership. Material success alone fails to satisfy them; the prospect of aging frightens them; and in an increasingly fast-paced, impersonal world, they struggle to find a sense of belonging. Despite their personal problems, however, Simon's characters are essentially likable; indeed, audiences readily identify with these imperfect, unheroic figures who are at heart decent human beings.

Although Simon did not emphasize the Jewishness of his characters in his early plays—creating instead a basic "urban type"[9]—he has focused more openly on his Jewish heritage during the last two decades, presenting characters in plays such as the Brighton Beach trilogy and *Lost in Yonkers* who are explicitly Jewish. Members of other ethnic minorities rarely figure in Simon's plays. Hispanic characters, such as the Spanish Costazuela brothers in the female version of *The Odd Couple* (1985), have relatively minor roles, and *Proposals* (1997) is Simon's only play featuring a major character who is African American. Female characters in Simon's comedies are typically presented in traditional roles of wives and mothers (e.g., Corie Bratter in *Barefoot in the Park* and Kate Jerome in *Broadway Bound*). Those women who manage to have successful careers outside the home, like Maggie in *Jake's Women,* are rarely pictured as happy; indeed, most of Simon's women seem to find it difficult to live without a man. Similarly, the author's male characters, like Felix Ungar in *The Odd Couple* or Jake in *Jake's Women,* are often shown to be dependent on the women in their lives.

Simon's style of comedy can be traced back to Menander (342?–291? B.C.E.), the master of Greek New Comedy. Credited with writing more than one hundred plays (of which only one survives in its entirety), Menander helped to replace the Old Comedy of Aristophanes with a more realistic comedy of manners. He refined the use of stock characters, blended humorous and tragic themes, and focused his comedies on domestic life rather than the public arena. Strongly influencing the Roman comedies of Plautus and Terence, and through them the comedies of Shakespeare and many modern playwrights, Menander's plays have also left their mark on the romantic comedies of the movies.

The plots of most of Simon's comedies follow a basic storyline derived from Menander. According to Northrop Frye, "What normally happens is that a young man wants a young woman, that his desire is resisted by some opposition, usually paternal, and that near the end of the play some twist in the plot enables the hero to have his will."[10] In many of his comedies, however, Simon presents a variation of this boy-meets-girl plot in which the protagonists are already married and their love is starting to fade for some reason. His characters are often tempted to break their wedding vows or to separate because of marital difficulties, but in the end they manage to reaffirm their mutual commitment. Simon's comedies, too, typically conclude not with the celebration of a new marriage but with the renewal of an old one.

Although one of the classical functions of comedy has been to advocate the need for social change, Simon is not overtly political in his approach to playwriting. The closest he comes to social commentary is probably in *The Prisoner of Second Avenue* (1971), in which the protagonist, Mel Edison, is outraged by urban ills such as crime, pollution, and unemployment. When Simon depicts a political leftist, as he does in *Broadway Bound* in the person of the protagonist's grandfather, Ben, the man is not a heroic figure but simply a harmless old socialist who admires Trotsky. Even in *Laughter on the 23rd Floor,* a play set during the hysteria of the McCarthy era, the political issues are secondary to the comic wit and behavior of the characters themselves—a group of television comedy writers and their eccentric star. Rather than confronting society in a political manner through his comedies, Simon is simply interested in showing human beings as they are—with their foibles, eccentricities, and absurdities.

One of the most important influences on Simon is his Jewish heritage, particularly the tradition of Jewish humor to which he belongs. Simon does not consciously set out to write Jewish humor, but he acknowledges that his Jewish background is "so deeply embedded in me and so inherent in me that I am unaware of its quality."[11] As Daniel Walden explains, "Modern American Jewish humor has its roots in the humor of the *shtetlach,* the Jewish ghettoes of Eastern Europe. Based on a recognition of the power of the surrounding community and the helplessness of the Jews, it fused sentiment with irony and self-satire with earthiness. Alienated from the mainstream, pressured to convert, lacerated by persecutions and pogroms, Jews in the nineteenth century used religion, folklore, fantasy, mysticism, and humor to survive, and, almost miraculously, flourish."[12]

A common element of Jewish humor is an attitude of martyrdom and self-pity. In *The Prisoner of Second Avenue,* for example, after Mel Edison is fired from his job, he tells his wife, "I thought maybe another job would turn up, a miracle would happen . . . Miracles don't happen when you're forty-seven . . . When Moses saw the burning bush, he must have been twenty-three, twenty-four, the most. Never forty-seven."[13] Eugene Jerome in *Brighton Beach Memoirs* (1983) likewise adopts this martyrlike attitude when he declares that he hates his name: "How am I ever going to play for the Yankees with a name like Eugene Morris Jerome? You have to be a Joe . . . or a Tony . . . or Frankie . . . If only I was born Italian . . . All the best Yankees are Italian . . . My mother makes spaghetti with ketchup, what chance do I have?"[14]

Traditional Jewish humor is also self-deprecating, with the oppressed Jews making themselves the butt of the joke. In the Brighton Beach trilogy Eugene Jerome is a master of this self-deprecating form of humor, cleverly poking fun at himself and at his Jewish culture as a whole. In *Broadway Bound,* for instance, Eugene explains that when he went ice skating with his girlfriend, he fell down repeatedly and returned home chilled and feverish. "Jewish guys are never good at sports played between November and April," he explains. When his mother tells him how her grandparents cried when they first saw the Statue of Liberty because she wasn't a Jewish woman, Eugene responds, "That would be a riot. A Jewish Statue of Liberty. In her left hand, she'd be holding a baking pan . . . and in the right hand, held up high, the electric bill."[15]

The ultimate goal of such self-deprecating humor is to transcend one's status as victim—to prevail, to flourish. As Sarah Blacher Cohen suggests, Jewish humor has actually been a means of salvation: "It has helped the Jewish people to survive, to confront the indifferent, often hostile universe, to endure the painful ambiguities of life and to retain a sense of internal power despite external impotence."[16] Simon's own brand of humor, which, in the playwright's words, "is often self-deprecating and usually sees life from the grimmest point of view,"[17] belongs to a tradition of Jewish humor that includes Saul Bellow, Bernard Malamud, and Philip Roth—a tradition which values laughter as a defense mechanism and which sees humor as a healing, life-giving force. According to

Daniel Walden, Simon's Jewish-style comedies resonate with Jews and gentiles alike, because Simon recognizes that the figure of the suffering, self-doubting Jew is "a twentieth-century symbol for Everyman. . . . Alienation, acculturation, and assimilation, allegedly Jewish diseases, belong to all, just as the humor that emanates from the tensions is universal."[18]

Simon's comedies are also semi-autobiographical, influenced by experiences such as the author's troubled childhood and his first two marriages. "I suppose you could practically trace my life through my plays," Simon admits. "They always come out of what I'm thinking about and what I am as a person."[19] In his first comedy, *Come Blow Your Horn,* Simon simply wrote about what he knew best: himself, his parents, and his brother, Danny. Later in his career, however, he began to use his plays as a way of understanding himself and the world around him—sometimes writing autobiographically for cathartic reasons, as he did in *Chapter Two* (1977), a play inspired by the death of his first wife, Joan—or for the purpose of self-analysis, as he did in the expressionistic *Jake's Women,* in which he invites the audience to share in the mind of a writer.

Another important aspect of Simon's autobiographical approach is his preoccupation with the past. According to Michael Woolf, "a characteristic of American-Jewish culture appears to be a continued necessity to revisit past experience, to return repeatedly to one form or another of history" (e.g., persecution in Europe, the immigration experience, the Depression, and the Holocaust).[20] As a writer of comedy, Simon offers his audiences a softened view of history—especially in *Brighton Beach Memoirs,* in which he nostalgically recalls his childhood during the Depression, creating what one reviewer termed a "love letter to his past."[21] For Simon, coming to terms with the past, both in a cultural and personal sense, helps him to understand and cope with the realities of contemporary life. As his character George Schneider remarks in *Chapter Two,* "You can't get to the present without going through the past."[22]

One of the most interesting tensions in Simon's plays is that between realism and comedy. As a realist, Simon is determined to create characters who are lifelike and convincing; but as a writer of comedy, he wants these individuals to be broadly humorous. Thus he must provide his characters with amusing dialogue and exaggerated traits (e.g., Felix Ungar's obsessive neatness and Oscar Madison's extreme sloppiness in *The Odd Couple*); at the same time, Simon must transcend comic stereotypes, leaving the audience with the impression that these characters are living human beings. In his first Broadway play, *Come Blow Your Horn,* Simon relied almost exclusively on type characters: the playboy, the naive young man, the Jewish mother. But one character—the father, Harry Baker—rose above such stereotypes to become the most convincing, as well as the most interesting, character in the play. In his portrait of Baker, at least, Simon managed to create a delicate balance between realism and comedy—an achievement that he strove to repeat in his later plays.

The tension between realism and comedy in Simon's work is most conspicuous in the endings to his plays. Like virtually any writer of comedy, Simon wants to conclude his dramas with a sense of harmony, reconciliation, and optimism. But he is also drawn to an ending that is more realistic—an *open* ending in which the problems of the characters are not completely resolved, an ending which may even be tinged by sadness. During the early part of his career, Simon was more inclined to employ a traditionally happy ending—sometimes to the detriment of his work, as in the conclusion to *The Odd Couple,* in which the reconciliation between Felix and Oscar is forced and unconvincing. Later, however, he became more adept at offering a modified happy ending—especially in some of his most skillfully crafted plays, such as *The Sunshine Boys, Broadway Bound,* and *Lost in Yonkers.* Curiously enough, Simon's efforts to provide his comedies with happy endings have frequently been castigated by critics, who clearly are looking for more realism in his work and who have accused him on occasion of "Pollyannaism."

Although he is not a philosophical playwright, Simon does reveal a basic view of the world, as well as a fundamental set of values, some of which have been shared by writers of comedy since the time of the ancient Greeks. First of all, Simon believes in moderation, compromise—the golden mean. This belief is reflected in his portraits of long-term relationships, in which pairs of individuals must effect a compromise (e.g., in *Barefoot in the Park, The Odd Couple,* and *The Sunshine Boys*), as well as in his depictions of hedonistic characters whose excesses need to be cured (e.g., Alan Baker in *Come Blow Your Horn* and Barney Cashman in *Last of the Red Hot Lovers*). Besides supporting moderation, Simon upholds the importance of social norms, emphasizing not the primacy of the individual but the human need for community. Comparing Simon with Menander, Arvid F. Sponberg argues that both playwrights "assume that humans in social settings will strive to conform to the norms of society, and each writer takes the value of those norms to be self-evident. . . . Setting oneself above or below the norm, or apart from it, invites justifiable ridicule."[23]

Simon believes strongly in the institution of marriage—the ultimate symbol of social harmony—and in the importance of the family unit. Despite the marital problems of his parents and his own history of divorce (from his second wife, Marsha Mason, in 1982 and from his third wife, Diane Lander, in 1988 and again ten years later), Simon repeatedly suggests in his plays that a loving marriage and a close-knit family can offer genuine fulfillment. Promiscuity and infidelity do not lead to happiness—as illustrated by Evy Meara in *The Gingerbread Lady,* Marvin Michaels in *California Suite,* and Leo Schneider in *Chapter Two.* And when Simon's characters are deprived of a healthy family structure, as in *Lost in Yonkers,* they end up emotionally damaged and "lost."

Simon also shares with other writers of comedy a basic sense of affirmation—a faith in human survival. His characters suffer from a variety of woes and sometimes are overwhelmed by their problems; yet life goes on for them. At the end of *The Odd Couple,* after Oscar Madison has quarreled with the compulsively neat Felix Ungar and has evicted him from the apartment, Oscar asks Felix if he will at least return next Friday for their usual poker game. "You're not going to break up the game, are you?" he says. "Me? Never!" answers Felix. "Marriages may come and go, but the game must go on."[24] Similarly, at the close of *Lost in Yonkers,* when Jay and Arty's father returns to take the boys away from their grandmother's house, the older brother, Jay, declares, "We made it, Arty. Ten months here and we're still alive. We got through Grandma and we're all right."[25]

Yet Simon's faith in human survival—his sense of comic joy— is invariably colored by sadness. The author once explained his comic vision as follows: "Arthur Miller says in his plays 'how tragic life is' and thank God for playwrights like him. . . . My view is 'how sad and funny life is.' I can't think of a humorous situation that does

not involve some pain. I used to ask, 'What is a funny situation?'
Now I ask, 'What is a sad situation and how can I tell it humorously?'"[26] This Chekhovian mixture of humor and poignancy—of
laughter and tears—is a hallmark of Simon's comedy. Reviewing
Simon's autobiographical play *Chapter Two,* Richard Eder pointed
out that "Neil Simon's popularity rests upon his fine control of a
very particular kind of painful comedy. It consists of his characters
saying and doing funny things in ludicrous contrast to the unhappiness they are feeling."[27] Again, this notion is very much related to
Jewish humor and the use of laughter as a defense mechanism.

During the last thirty years Simon's comedies have gradually
grown more serious. Plays like *Broadway Bound,* in which Simon
confronts the pain of his parents' marital breakup, and *Lost in
Yonkers,* in which he deals with emotional abuse in a highly dysfunctional family, are a far cry from the comedic fluff of *Come Blow
Your Horn* and *Barefoot in the Park*—delightful as that fluff might
be. But if one examines the author's entire canon, one recognizes
that Simon has always addressed serious themes—for example,
marital conflict, infidelity, divorce, sibling rivalry, adolescence,
bereavement, and fear of aging. In several plays Simon has even
dealt with issues as troubling as alcoholism, homophobia, and anti-
Semitism. As a writer of comedy, however, the playwright has chosen to treat these themes in an amusing manner—to take a painful
subject and "tell it humorously."

Simon also suggests that by focusing on the painful aspects of
human experience, he ultimately transcends the pain, arriving at a
sense of connection, a feeling of shared humanity: "I grew up seeing the torment of broken families, broken lives, and broken hearts,
and although I always found the absurdity of how we live our lives,

I always looked for the pain when I wrote about it. Writing about it in a play or on this page doesn't lessen the pain, but it allows you to look at it from a distance, objectively instead of subjectively, and you begin to see a common truth that connects us all."[28]

CHAPTER TWO

Come Blow Your Horn and *Barefoot in the Park*

Come Blow Your Horn

Neil Simon's first Broadway play did not come easily. It was a project that took over three years to complete, with two and one-half years spent on revisions. By the time he finished *Come Blow Your Horn* (1961) Simon had written twenty-two entire drafts, working on all of these versions while earning his living as a comedy writer for television. As Simon explained, writing this play was basically a declaration of independence, a way of breaking free from his brother, Danny, and striking out professionally on his own: "After an entire childhood of idolizing him, learning from him, fearing him, respecting him, and loving him, I was also beginning to feel dominated by him and I had an urgent need to separate from him, to become, in a term not yet then in fashion, my own person."[1]

Come Blow Your Horn is an autobiographical comedy recalling the period when Neil and Danny Simon left their parents' home for the first time to live in their own apartment. Although the play contains some of the elements of the classic Menandrian boy-meets-girl plot, it primarily focuses on the theme of coming of age. Alan Baker, based on Danny Simon, is a suave bachelor and womanizer who stands in sharp contrast to his naive younger brother, Buddy, modeled on the playwright. Describing Buddy's initial experiences as a "swinging" bachelor and Alan's first serious romance, the play centers on the brothers' efforts to break free from their parents—especially from the tyrannical control of their father, Harry. In the end, however, it is only Alan Baker who truly comes into his manhood.

The family in the play is not specifically identified as Jewish, but the characters' speech patterns and values tend to reflect Simon's Jewish heritage. Consider the Yiddish cadences in the following outburst from the father, Harry Baker: "May you and your brother live and be well. God bless you, all the luck in the world, you should know nothing but happiness. If I ever speak to either one of you again, my tongue should fall out!"[2] Likewise, Mrs. Baker—with her zealous devotion to her family, her interest in matchmaking, and her fetish about cleanliness—is a version of the stereotypical Jewish mother. Indeed, despite the fact that the family's name is Baker, critic Ellen Schiff views *Come Blow Your Horn* as "the embryo of the explicitly Jewish *Brighton Beach Memoirs*," which Simon was to write more than two decades later.[3]

The Baker brothers, Alan and Buddy, are initially pictured as opposites—the first in a series of "odd couples" that Simon would later present in his comedies. At thirty-three, Alan is smooth, worldly, and experienced with women. When the play opens, he is shown returning from a trip to Vermont with the sexy (but not very bright) Peggy Evans and is glibly trying to entice her into his apartment. Alan has a more serious attachment with a woman named Connie Dayton, but he has made it clear to Connie that he relishes his bachelor life and is not yet ready to consider marriage. In contrast to Alan, Buddy Baker is portrayed as quiet, shy, and unsure of himself. At twenty-one, he is still inexperienced with women, admitting that it took him three months just to get a date for his prom. "Look, there's a big difference between the way you and I operate," he tells his brother. "If I get a handshake from a girl I figure I had a good night" (47).

Simon emphasizes the contrast in personality between Alan and Buddy in order to introduce the play's fundamental theme of maturation. Buddy, in fact, has already made a first step toward manhood at the start of the drama. He has left his parents' home for good and has come to live with Alan in his apartment. Hoping to become a writer some day, Buddy is also making plans to leave the family business (a company that manufactures wax fruit), even though this action will inevitably anger and disappoint his father. Impressed by his younger brother's resolve, Alan seeks to accelerate Buddy's passage into manhood by offering him Peggy Evans as a birthday present, persuading Buddy to impersonate a Hollywood producer in order to win Peggy's sexual favors.

Simon's coming-of-age theme is reinforced by the ancient comedic device of the exchange of identities. Much to Alan's dismay, Buddy learns the freewheeling bachelor's game all too quickly, eventually turning into a mirror image of his playboy brother. In act 3, after having shared Alan's apartment for several weeks, Buddy exudes a surprising confidence that borders on brashness. He has quit his job and has been staying out late every night, meeting women with exotic names like "Snow Eskanazi" and enjoying the pleasures of a "swinging" bachelor's life. Realizing that Buddy's independence has led to irresponsibility and self-indulgence, Alan is forced to examine his own bachelor lifestyle and to reevaluate his notion of what it really means to be a man. He begins to lose his earlier bravado, growing more serious and insecure—the way his younger brother used to be.

Just as Alan Baker represents one model for manhood—reflecting independence, adventure, and sexual potency—so does the father, Harry Baker, represent another. For Harry, manhood means having a sense of responsibility, especially to one's family. It means being married, raising children, and working hard to support them. It means adhering to traditional values. The problem for both Alan and Buddy, however, is that Harry forces his beliefs on his sons in a heavy-handed manner and refuses to acknowledge their own need for freedom. After berating Alan for his irresponsibility at work and the excesses in his personal life, Harry calls him a bum for not being married. He likewise fails to understand why Buddy, at twenty-one, would want to move away from home and quit his job making wax fruit. Even when Buddy discloses his dream of writing dramas for television or the theater, Harry says, "Plays can close . . . Television you turn off. Wax fruit lays in the bowl till you're a hundred" (67).

The play's title, *Come Blow Your Horn,* is derived from the well-known nursery rhyme about Little Boy Blue, the youth who fell asleep while tending his livestock. Just as the nursery rhyme is a call to responsibility, so is Simon's comedy. Indeed, by the end of the drama, the older brother, Alan Baker, answers such a call. He proposes marriage to his girlfriend, Connie; makes up for his negligence at work by arranging several profitable business deals; and also manages—somewhat miraculously—to reconcile with his domineering father. Although this conversion might strike audiences as sudden and contrived, Alan has apparently discovered that manhood involves more than independence and sexual prowess. He is ready now to moderate his habits, to become a responsible adult, and, without kowtowing to his father, to embrace the traditional values of his parents. Alan thus represents, in Simon's view, the final stage of maturation—integration with society. Buddy, on the other hand, has only taken the first step toward manhood—independence from his parents—and does not yet share his brother's more mature understanding. Awaiting his date with Snow Eskanazi at the end of the play, Buddy is still, to a large extent, an embodiment of Little Boy Blue.

As Edythe M. McGovern has noted, *Come Blow Your Horn* employs certain techniques found in "well-made" French farces— not only the previously-mentioned exchange of identities but also "French scenes," meaning that each time a character exits, another comes onstage, and a new scene commences.[4] In act 1, for example, Alan talks seductively with Peggy Evans, who leaves just before Buddy arrives at Alan's apartment. The brothers have a lengthy discussion until Buddy exits into the bedroom, whereupon their father, Harry Baker, arrives to scold Alan for not showing up for work. Although several scenes in the play involve three to five characters (e.g., Harry Baker's confrontation with the two brothers in act 2), *Come Blow Your Horn* is primarily written as a series of two-person scenes, thus allowing the audience to focus on the specific conflicts between each pair of characters.

The influence of television is also evident in Simon's first play. Like many situation comedies, Simon's drama has a thin plot, relying instead on clever one-liners and situational or visual gags for its humorous effect. One scene, in which a befuddled Mrs. Baker tries to take a series of telephone messages while furiously searching for a pencil, is even reminiscent of vaudeville. One of Simon's favorite devices in the play is a running gag that might be called "the surprise entrance": the doorbell rings, but the character at the door is not the person who is expected. In act 1, for instance, when Alan assumes that the sexy Peggy Evans is at the door, he opens it, only to find his father standing there, "scowling disgustedly" (25). In addition, Simon makes use of certain stock characters typically found in television comedy—for example, the bimbo, the rakish bachelor, and the doting mother. Although reviewers criticized Simon for his stock characters, such figures are, in fact, a basic staple of comedy, and Simon knew from his experience in television that they were certain to draw laughs from an audience.

When *Come Blow Your Horn* opened on Broadway in February 1961, critics pointed to weaknesses such as the play's thin subject matter and its stereotyped characters but essentially agreed that it was a lively comedy. Reviewing the play for the *New York Post,* Richard Watts Jr. wrote: "With a certain amount of reluctance, I must concede that much of 'Come Blow Your Horn' is entertaining. . . . The play, while always a trifle ramshackle, does keep growing in effectiveness and the third act is quite delightful. Nor can Mr. Simon's ability to write a good, amusing line be dismissed from attention."[5] Reviewers were nearly unanimous in their praise for the vivid characterization of Harry Baker, whose inflexibility and despotic treatment of his sons becomes comical. A success with the public, the play ran for nearly two years on Broadway, launching Simon's career as a dramatist.

Come Blow Your Horn is clearly the work of a fledgling playwright and cannot be numbered among Simon's better comedies. The plot lacks substance, and the characters, with a few exceptions, are not particularly memorable. But this play represents a promising start for Simon and helps readers appreciate his subsequent development as a dramatist. As Simon himself explained, "*Come Blow Your Horn* . . . , in the time it was written, seemed like a monumental effort. Today, it seems like the crude markings in a cave by the first prehistoric chronicler. Still, it was an important step for me. The theater and I discovered each other."[6]

Barefoot in the Park

Barefoot in the Park (1963) is a romantic comedy based on the early days of Simon's marriage to his first wife, Joan. The play basically follows the standard plot for romantic comedy established by Menander and employed by generations of writers ever since: boy meets girl; boy loses girl; boy wins girl. Simon, however, offers a variation of this ancient plot in which his characters, Paul and Corie Bratter, are a newlywed couple experiencing problems in their first week of marriage. As in most romantic comedies, the couple must overcome certain external and internal obstacles before their marriage can be restored to harmony. In particular, the Bratters must learn the value of moderation and compromise—the central theme of this lighthearted play.

A major obstacle that faces newlyweds Paul and Corie Bratter is their New York efficiency apartment, located on the fifth floor of an old brownstone building. Modeled on the first home that Simon and his wife shared after their marriage in 1953, the apartment is cramped, with a small dressing room serving as the bedroom. Forced to share an oversize single bed, Paul and Corie must "turn in unison" when they sleep.[7] The tiny bathroom has no tub, much to Paul's disappointment, and in the living room the couple even discovers a hole in the glass skylight that allows rain and snow to fall into their love nest.

Simon takes advantage of the comic possibilities presented by the apartment, particularly emphasizing the five flights of stairs that must be climbed in order to reach the Bratters' home. As Robert K. Johnson observes, the running gag of the stairs helps the audience gain insight into the characters by revealing their varied responses to the long climb.[8] Corie, who is young and exuberant, doesn't allow the stairs to affect her. Neither does her fifty-eight-year-old neighbor, Victor Velasco, who has a genuine zest for life. On the other hand, Paul Bratter and Corie's mother, Ethel Banks, who are much less carefree, stagger and gasp for air when they enter the apartment. Problems and responsibilities tend to weigh on their minds, and the stairs simply add to their overall sense of burden.

The primary obstacle facing the Bratters, however, is not external, but internal. Although Corie and Paul obviously love each other, they appear to be complete opposites in personality. Corie is a thorough romantic, a young woman who would like to prolong her honeymoon as much as possible. Eccentric, adventuresome, and impulsive, she is a free spirit whose idea of fun is to do something wild and crazy. Corie enjoys walking barefoot in the park in the winter, eating exotic food, and thinking of outrageous pranks to play on her neighbors. Paul, on the other hand, is conventional, conservative, and practical—a no-nonsense lawyer who has just been given his first case. So formal is Paul that Corie says she even wondered before they were married if he wore a tie to bed. In her view, her husband has no spirit of adventure and is too proper and dignified to know how to enjoy himself. "It's suddenly very clear that you and I have absolutely *nothing* in common" (178), she exclaims.

A typical feature of romantic comedy (especially the Shakespearean variety) that Simon employs in *Barefoot in the Park* is the inclusion of a second pair of lovers. The playwright uses Corie's mother, Ethel Banks, and the Bratters' neighbor, Victor Velasco, as reflector characters in order to accentuate the personality clash between the Bratters themselves. Mrs. Banks is a middle-aged, somewhat frumpy-looking woman who appears to have no real life of her own. Afraid to consider a new relationship with a man, she is distressed by the thought of going on a blind date with Victor Velasco. Like Paul, Mrs. Banks is conservative and cautious. She doesn't "jump into life" (131); she looks first. Victor Velasco, however, resembles the free-spirited Corie. He is adventuresome and impulsive, doing whatever gives him the most pleasure in life. At fifty-eight, Velasco enjoys skiing and mountain climbing and likes to cook exotic food. He has been married three times and still has a reputation as a ladies' man. Just as Corie and Paul prove to be an "odd couple," so, too, do Mrs. Banks and the debonair Velasco.

Besides including a second pair of lovers, Simon makes use of the ancient technique of the exchange of identities in order to move his comedy toward a happy conclusion. In act 2 Paul temporarily takes on some of Corie's eccentric traits, while Corie grows more serious and conventional. After having walked barefoot in the park in freezing weather, a drunken and feverish Paul returns to the apartment near the end of the play, crawling out on the ledge outside their bedroom window. Frightened by her husband's bizarre behavior, Corie suddenly realizes that she wants "the old Paul back" (211), that she needs him to take care of her, and that she loves him for being strong and reliable.

This exchange of identities might strike contemporary readers as implausible—particularly Corie's seeming transformation into a conventional, dependent wife. It must be remembered, however, that although Corie displays the free spirit of the liberated American female, she is at heart a traditional housewife of the 1950s—someone whose greatest joy is to create a loving home for her husband and her future children. Delighted that she is married, Corie refers to herself as "Mrs. Paul Bratter." When Victor Velasco asks her if she is a folk singer, she answers, "No. A wife" (138). Corie's response at the end of the play is perfectly in keeping, therefore, with her sense of herself as a homemaker. She will fix up their apartment, she will make their home as comfortable as possible, and she will enjoy the security of Paul's love. Earlier in the play Corie's mother advised her to "give up a little of you for him. . . . Take care of him. And make him feel important. And if you can do that, you'll have a happy and wonderful marriage" (207). "Giving up a little of herself" is exactly what Corie is trying to do at the end of the play.

The exchange of identities also provides a better understanding of Paul Bratter's character and makes clear his willingness to compromise. In reality Paul is not a boring conformist or "stuffed shirt." His sudden impulse to walk barefoot in the park confirms his capacity to engage in unconventional behavior and to appreciate spontaneity in others. Indeed, earlier in the play, Paul is shown to have a good imagination and a quick sense of humor. In act 1, when Corie tells him that she wants to do "something wild, insane, and crazy" the next night, he answers, "Well . . . I'll come home early and we'll wallpaper each other" (117). In act 2, when Corie says that she used to imagine him sleeping with a tie, he quips, "No, no. Just for very *formal* sleeps" (176). Paul is clearly drawn to Corie's impulsiveness and quirky charm. She brings out the playfulness, the good humor in his own personality, and Simon implies that she will continue to do so long after the honeymoon is over.

A similar exchange of identities takes place between the secondary characters, Ethel Banks and Victor Velasco. While Mrs. Banks becomes more carefree and adventuresome, Velasco grows more practical and conservative. Their blind date—a night out on the town together with Paul and Corie—is marred by a variety of mishaps, but both Mrs. Banks and Velasco learn something important from the experience. Mrs. Banks realizes that it is all right for her to have a little fun and adventure in her life—that she is still "a young, vital woman" (134). Victor Velasco, on the other hand, discovers that he is not as young as he thought he was and that he must moderate his habits in the future. He tells Mrs. Banks, "Last night I couldn't carry you up the stairs. I can't eat rich foods any more . . . (Very confidentially) . . . and I dye my hair" (203). As Edythe M. McGovern notes, "In a very real sense each of the four characters has altered his behavior so that it has become less polarized, less radical, less extreme. Each person has gravitated toward a moderation which seems to be the playwright's ideal."[9]

In *Barefoot in the Park* Simon supports not only moderation and compromise but also the institution of marriage itself. His faith in marriage is revealed by the reconciliation that takes place between Corie and Paul at the end of the play and by the rapprochement between Ethel Banks and Victor Velasco that brings these characters into the same sphere of social harmony. A minor character—the telephone repair man, Harry Pepper—also voices Simon's optimism about marriage when he remarks, "With all the trouble today, you see a couple of newlyweds, you figure there's still hope for the world" (189).

The earliest of Simon's collaborations with director Mike Nichols (who won the Tony Award for Best Director), *Barefoot in the Park* (1963) was an instant hit with both the critics and the public, enjoying a run on Broadway that lasted for almost four years.

Howard Taubman, reviewing the play for the *New York Times,* called it a "bubbling, rib-tickling comedy" and claimed that Simon exhibited "the dash of a highly skilled professional writer."[10] Norman Nadel, in the *New York World-Telegram and The Sun,* wrote that "Simon's scintillating dialogue, the cast's spirited playing and Nichols' clear genius as a director of comedy turn this [play] into the merriest evening Broadway has enjoyed in years."[11] John McClain of the *Journal-American* summed up the response of many playgoers when he remarked that *Barefoot in the Park* was, quite simply, the funniest comedy he had ever seen.[12]

As Bonamy Dobrée has argued, classical comedy, from which a great deal of modern comedy is derived, "tends to repress eccentricity, exaggeration, any deviation from the normal. . . . From Terence to the present day, it supports the happy mean."[13] In *Come Blow Your Horn* and *Barefoot in the Park* Simon takes just such a stand against excess, firmly aligning himself with this golden mean—and, in the process, giving his audiences some of the liveliest humor since the Broadway hits of Moss Hart and George S. Kaufman.

CHAPTER THREE

The Odd Couple

Simon originally conceived of *The Odd Couple* (1965) as a black comedy—a play that would represent a clear departure from the lighthearted entertainment of *Come Blow Your Horn* and *Barefoot in the Park.*[1] The central premise of *The Odd Couple* is, after all, a fairly serious one: two men who are separated from their spouses try sharing an apartment, only to discover that they cannot get along any better with each other than they did with their wives. When he began the play, Simon was actually thinking about the problem of divorce "and about two men who are basically unhappy."[2] What he ended up with was a classic portrait of incompatibility as well as an amusing study of sexual stereotypes.

The Odd Couple was inspired by the experience of Simon's brother, Danny, who, after the breakup of his nine-year marriage, moved in with a theatrical agent and friend named Roy Gerber. Though the relations between the new roommates were normally cordial, Danny was angered when Roy and his friends would arrive late for the meals he had cooked; once, when their dates for the evening were a full hour late because of Roy's negligence, "Danny almost killed Roy with his spatula."[3] Recognizing the humor of this bizarre domestic situation, Simon decided to exaggerate the differences between the men until the two characters in his play were complete opposites, unable to live compatibly in the same apartment or even to get along in any situation. The result was not the black comedy that Simon initially imagined but a humorous play that does, nonetheless, have a serious edge to it.

THE ODD COUPLE

Although *The Odd Couple* is not a romantic comedy like *Barefoot in the Park,* it makes use of the same "problem marriage" framework found in the earlier play and in this sense offers a clever variation of the classical Menandrian plot. *The Odd Couple* concerns two heterosexual males who enter into a new domestic partnership, just as Paul and Corie Bratter entered into a new marriage. Oscar and Felix are themselves aware that this new living arrangement is a "marriage," of sorts. When Oscar invites Felix to move into his apartment, he quips, "For crying out loud, I'm proposing to you. What do you want, a ring?"[4] At various points in the play the two men call each other by their wives' names—either jokingly or by accident. And when Oscar finally evicts Felix from his apartment, he exclaims, "I want you out of here. Now! Tonight! . . . It's all over, Felix. The whole marriage. We're getting an annulment!" (291).

As Ruby Cohn has noted, the technique of using "a comically contrasting pair [of characters] is at least as old as Plautus, with his Menachmus brothers, and that device was undoubtedly reinforced by the two-brother structure of Simon's own family."[5] Oscar Madison and Felix Ungar are unquestionably an odd couple. Oscar, a successful sportswriter, is sloppy, easy-going, and unreliable. Recently divorced, he is eight hundred dollars behind in his alimony payments and owes money to his friends as well. His New York apartment—"a study in slovenliness" (217)—is littered with dirty dishes, glasses, newspapers, mail, and cast-off clothing. Furthermore, the refrigerator is broken, the air conditioner doesn't work, and the maid quit because the job got to be too much for her. Yet Oscar still plays the role of amiable host at the weekly poker game with his buddies. When the other men grumble about the messy apartment or the stale refreshments, he simply laughs and explains that the green sandwiches are "either very new cheese or very old meat" (221).

In contrast to his friend Oscar, Felix Ungar is compulsively neat, fastidious, and high-strung—the two men forming a radically incongruous pair. Felix confesses that he used to clean his apartment after both the maid and his wife, Frances, had finished working on it. "I can't help it. I like things clean" (246), he explains. He also admits making constant adjustments to his wife's cooking—convinced that he himself is the better cook. Unlike the easy-going Oscar, Felix is nervous, hypochondriac, and at times hysterical. Indeed, his poker buddies are greatly worried when they learn that Felix's marriage has broken up, that Felix has been missing for twenty-four hours, and that he sent his wife a suicide telegram. Murray remarks, "He'll go to pieces. I know Felix. He's going to try something crazy" (230).

Simon's exaggeration of the differences between Oscar and Felix is typical of the comic mode. According to Robert B. Heilman, "In comedy there is a constant awareness of the discordant"—whether this be the discrepancy between illusion and reality, between character and situation, or between two characters whom the audience views simultaneously. Heilman adds that "incongruity hinges often upon the idea of a compelling norm from which we would not willingly defect."[6] In the case of *The Odd Couple* that implied norm is a middle ground between Oscar and Felix—a delicate balance between freedom and discipline, between spontaneity and order. *The Odd Couple* can be seen, in fact, as a natural outgrowth of Simon's first two plays, *Come Blow Your Horn* and *Barefoot in the Park,* both of which clearly embrace the idea of the golden mean.

The poker players themselves—Speed, Vinnie, Roy, and Murray—serve as a kind of Greek chorus who support this golden mean.[7] In act 1, for instance, before Oscar appears on stage, the men begin to remark on their host's slovenly habits. They complain about the stench in Oscar's apartment, about the broken air conditioner, about the litter that surrounds them, and about the spoiled food that Oscar tries to serve them. During act 2, after Felix has turned Oscar's apartment into an immaculate, sterile environment (even washing and disinfecting the playing cards), some of the poker players are equally critical of Felix's behavior. "I've had it up to here," Speed complains. "In the last three hours we played four minutes of poker. I'm not giving up my Friday nights to watch cooking and housekeeping" (254). In their role as Greek chorus, the poker players thus emerge as a voice for moderation. Uncomfortable with the extreme behavior of both Oscar and Felix, these average citizens implicitly affirm the need for a middle course.

Although Simon was interested in exploring some serious themes in *The Odd Couple,* the play actually takes on many aspects of buffoon comedy. According to Paul H. Grawe, "In buffoon comedy, our attention centers on a figure whose foibles and eccentricities are constantly threatening to undo him. By a variety of technical means, however, the author [persuades] us to respond sympathetically to this character and somehow to see him as representative of mankind in general."[8] In Simon's play we in fact have a pair of buffoons—two individuals whose habits are so extreme that they are each impossible to live with. Yet the audience not only laughs at the men's eccentric failings but also views Oscar and Felix in a sympathetic light. In this bizarrely incompatible pair, theatergoers see something of themselves—their marriages, their friendships, their own human failures. Indeed, the play rings so true that, as Robert K. Johnson notes, "Oscar Madison and Felix Ungar—and Simon's whole concept of 'the odd couple'—have become as much a part of our cultural folklore as Babbitt, Superman, Holden Caulfield, and Archie Bunker."[9]

Buffoon comedy, as Grawe suggests, tends to be more brutal than other dramatic types, often employing scenes of farcical violence: "Pie fights and other skirmishes in which the buffoon not only takes but returns exaggerated insult and injury are common."[10] Act 3 of *The Odd Couple,* in which Oscar and Felix find themselves in a state of open warfare, makes use of such brutal buffoonery. Incensed that Felix has ruined their double date with Oscar's neighbors, Gwendolyn and Cecily Pigeon, Oscar not only wrecks havoc on his own apartment, throwing a plate of linguini against the kitchen wall, but also chases Felix around the sofa, threatening to attack him. Such violent buffoonery signals a desire on Oscar's part to take charge again of his own apartment and his own life. After all, Felix has completely controlled Oscar for the last few weeks, nagging him about his personal habits and turning Oscar's apartment into a sterile showpiece—something out of "*House and Garden*" (268).

According to Grawe, buffoon comedy rarely concludes with the buffoon's complete victory over his antagonists or his unhappy circumstances, and Simon's play is no exception.[11] Oscar succeeds in evicting Felix from his home, yet he feels guilty about this seemingly callous treatment of a friend. Similarly, Felix is successful in finding temporary shelter with the Pigeon sisters, but he faces an uncertain future as a newly divorced man. Like most buffoon comedies, *The Odd Couple* pictures its main characters as loners, suggesting that integration with society (i.e., through the revitalization of a marriage) is not a viable alternative for them. Oscar and Felix were not able to live compatibly with their wives, nor could they get along any better with each other. In fact, aside from the weekly poker game with their friends, these characters appear to enjoy little sense of community.

The actual conclusion to *The Odd Couple* proves to be a somewhat disappointing blend of comedy and realism. In aiming for a comic resolution, the playwright unfortunately forces his protagonists to change too drastically, sacrificing consistency of character. Felix is suddenly not as shy and inhibited as he was before (as evidenced by his willingness to stay with the Pigeon sisters). Likewise, Oscar becomes more disciplined and responsible, paying the alimony checks that he owes to his wife and warning the other poker players not to drop cigarette butts on his rug. The problem with such changes is that Oscar and Felix have previously been depicted as characters who are extremely set in their ways. Not only are they opposite in personality and behavior, they are incapable of compromise. This inflexibility, this inability to change or to learn from past mistakes, is, in fact, a major reason for the failure of both men's marriages.

Besides exploring the issue of incompatibility in *The Odd Couple,* Simon also comments on sexual stereotypes. At the opening of the play Oscar's home is specifically pictured as a masculine domain. Cluttered and sloppy, the living room is said to have been "without the touch and care of a woman these past few months" (217). This masculine atmosphere is reinforced by Simon's use of the poker game ritual. Clearly, it is a "boys' night out" at Oscar's apartment, a time for cards, liquor, and male bonding. Not only are women unwelcome at the poker games, but the men also seem relieved to have escaped from their spouses. As Oscar says, "If I wanted nagging I'd go back with my wife" (220).

The arrival of Felix Ungar at Oscar's apartment signals an invasion of this masculine world by a distinctly feminine presence. Even when Simon was choosing the names for his two main characters, he apparently had male/female stereotypes in mind. He selected the name Oscar, he said, with its hard K sound, because it made him think of a strong, dominating individual; conversely, he chose the name Felix because he wanted a "prissy" name, and this one "sounded like a cartoon character, a shy and finicky person."[12] In act 1 of *The Odd Couple,* when the poker players are waiting for Felix to arrive, they introduce certain of his so-called "feminine" traits: (1) he is excessively neat (even cleaning the ashtrays at the poker games); (2) he is an excellent cook (known for dainty sandwiches such as cream cheese and pimento on date-nut bread); and (3) he is highly emotional and capable of hysterical outbursts. Even before Felix appears onstage, therefore, the audience is well aware of his stereotypically feminine qualities.

In writing *The Odd Couple,* Simon was probably influenced by one of his favorite plays—Tennessee Williams's *A Streetcar Named Desire* (1947)—a drama that contains two important poker scenes and that was originally entitled "The Poker Night." Oscar might be viewed, in fact, as an over-the-hill Stanley Kowalski; for at forty-three, Oscar, like Kowalski, is masculine and down-to-earth, enjoying "his weekly poker game, his friends, his excessive drinking and his cigars" (220). Just as Stanley Kowalski's poker game is interrupted by the return of his wife, Stella, and the fragile Southern belle, Blanche DuBois, so is Oscar's game interrupted, first by a phone call from his ex-wife (also named Blanche), then by the arrival of Felix Ungar, the frustrated homemaker who in some ways becomes a comical version of Oscar's former spouse. Both dramas thus depict the intrusion of the feminine into a thoroughly masculine realm, conveying the message that "poker shouldn't be played in a house with women."[13]

When writing the poker scene for act 2, Simon may also have been influenced by George S. Kaufman's one-act comedy *If Men Played Cards As Women Do* (1923), in which the game of poker has been completely feminized. Kaufman's play depicts a group of men who gather at a friend's apartment for a poker game that they never actually get around to playing. The host, John, is using his best china and filigree doilies and has even baked a cake for the occasion. The men compliment each other on their appearances and exchange gossip about love and marriage. They offer redecorating tips to the host, chatter about recipes, and discuss a sale on nightgowns at Lord & Taylor. Like his idol, Kaufman, Simon recognized the humor that could result when gender roles were reversed and "men played cards as women do." During the second poker game, in which Felix plays the role of attentive hostess—making elegant sandwiches and insisting on cleanliness—Simon basically makes use of the same stereotypes and incongruities that Kaufman employed in his comedy.

Felix is not, however, the only feminine presence to invade the "man's world" of Oscar's apartment. Although they never appear onstage, the wives of the poker players exert a strong influence over the men, at times controlling their husbands' behavior. Oscar's ex-wife, Blanche, telephones to remind the protagonist about his overdue alimony payments. Murray's wife calls to ask what time her husband will be home and to request that he bring her a corned beef sandwich and malted milk. Vinnie's wife insists that Vinnie leave the poker game by midnight, prompting him to check the time repeatedly. But it is Felix's wife, Frances, who has the most dominating presence of these unseen characters. Felix, in fact, cannot stop talking about the woman who wants to divorce him, even calling Oscar "Frances" by mistake when he bids Oscar good night at the close of act 1.

The masculine world of Oscar's apartment is also invaded by two female characters who do appear onstage: the British sisters Gwendolyn and Cecily Pigeon. These women (whose first names may have been borrowed from Oscar Wilde's *The Importance of Being Earnest*) draw out Felix's sensitive side and fill Oscar's home with an atmosphere of feminine emotion. When the ladies arrive for dinner in act 2, they listen sympathetically to Felix's tearful account of his marital breakup, crying as they recall the unhappiness of their own failed marriages and turning the double date that Oscar has planned into a general lamentation. At the end of the play the Pigeon sisters also interrupt the final poker game, coming to collect Felix's belongings after Oscar has evicted his roommate and injecting into this world of male bonding a spirit of motherly protection. "I just want to bundle him up in my arms and take care of him" (281), exclaims Cecily, referring to her desire to give Felix a temporary home. The "man's world" that Simon portrays in *The Odd Couple* is thus, in reality, not a masculine haven at all but a world that is constantly impinged on by women.

In her analysis of *The Odd Couple* Edythe M. McGovern argues that gender is not of special importance in the play: "It really does not matter that the two main characters, Oscar Madison and

THE ODD COUPLE

Felix Ungar . . . , are both men. They could be women, or they could be a married couple in the traditional sense."[14] The theme of incompatibility, of course, might be explored with any couple, regardless of gender. But much of the humor of Simon's play derives from male and female stereotypes and from the reversal of those stereotypes in the characterization of Felix Ungar. As Howard Taubman has observed, it is more amusing to see men imitating women than the other way around: "Women are bound to adore the sight of a man carrying on like a little homemaker. Men are sure to snicker at a male in domestic bondage to a man."[15] For comic purposes, therefore, it does matter that both Oscar and Felix are men.

The fact that *The Odd Couple* is—and should be—a comedy about men is illustrated by the relative inferiority of Simon's later "female" version of the play. Produced in 1985, twenty years after the original Broadway hit, this adaptation of *The Odd Couple* features two women characters, Olive Madison and Florence Ungar, who, like their male counterparts, try unsuccessfully to share an apartment after the breakup of their marriages. Although this newer version includes some humorous scenes—especially those involving the Costazuela brothers (the male equivalent of the Pigeon sisters)— the play as a whole is not as successful as its predecessor. Simon's feminization of the facts—for example, his substitution of Trivial Pursuit for the weekly poker game—is unsatisfying and gimmicky. More importantly, Simon is not able to use sexual stereotypes for humorous effect in the same way that he did in the male version of the play. It is not particularly funny, for instance, that Florence is a gourmet cook and a compulsive house cleaner, but it *is* amusing that Felix is. As a male, he is reversing a stereotype and acting unexpectedly. Reviewing the 1985 adaptation for the *Daily News,* Douglas Watt summed up the play's chief shortcoming: "What's missing in the female version of *The Odd Couple* is the oddity."[16]

Although *The Odd Couple* is not the black comedy that Simon originally planned to write, it clearly has more substance than the lighthearted *Come Blow Your Horn* or *Barefoot in the Park*—the latter of which Simon even referred to as "a soufflé."[17] Addressing subjects such as divorce, depression, friendship, and incompatibility, *The Odd Couple* is the first of Simon's comedies to confront serious issues and, in this sense, represents a turning point in the playwright's career. In a 1979 interview Simon admitted that until he wrote *The Odd Couple,* he had primarily been interested in getting laughs from his audiences. "But after *'The Odd Couple,'* I was convinced that I could make people laugh, so I no longer felt compelled to. . . . I've learned to protect the serious moments of my plays."[18] *The Odd Couple,* to be sure, is a classic portrait of incompatibility, as well as a study of sexual stereotypes. But it is also a play which affirms Simon's growing belief that comedy is a serious business.

CHAPTER FOUR

Plaza Suite and *Last of the Red Hot Lovers*

After *The Odd Couple* Simon continued his effort to produce a more serious brand of comedy, writing *Plaza Suite* (1968) and *Last of the Red Hot Lovers* (1969). Both plays are filled with amusing and even farcical moments, but they also explore a variety of serious themes, especially the tribulations of middle age. Presented as a group of one-acts (even though the latter play contains a single protagonist and is meant to be a full-length drama), these comedies demonstrate Simon's talent for creating innumerable variations of the ancient Menandrian boy-meets-girl plot, a plot that pervades the author's dramatic canon.

Plaza Suite

Plaza Suite (1968) is composed of three one-act plays, all set in the same suite of New York's Plaza Hotel. Not only do the plays have a common setting, but they are also united by common themes: marital conflict, infidelity, lack of communication, and fear of aging. Although each of these short plays is humorous, Simon viewed the first piece as a drama, the second as a comedy, and the third as a farce. Offering three different versions of the Menandrian boy-meets-girl plot, *Plaza Suite,* on the whole, presents a less sanguine view of marriage than is typical of classical comedy.

"Visitor from Mamaroneck"

"Visitor from Mamaroneck," like *Barefoot in the Park,* adopts a variation of the Menandrian plot that was especially popular in nineteenth-century French farces. As David Grote writes, "There, the lovers are often already married; the problem is that love is beginning to fade for some reason. Through a series of mistaken identities and false assumptions, the characters stray, pretend to stray, or prepare to stray until at the last moment order is restored, and all the confusions are cleared up."[1] In "Visitor from Mamaroneck," Simon introduces Sam and Karen Nash, a middle-aged couple who are experiencing difficulties in their marriage and who must confront the issue of infidelity. But instead of employing a typical Menandrian ending in which the couple's marriage is renewed, Simon opts for a more realistic and open-ended conclusion—an ending more in keeping with serious drama.

Reviewing the original production of *Plaza Suite,* Richard P. Cooke referred to Mamaroneck as "that suburban town in Westchester County often used synonymously with White Plains or Scarsdale as a seat of conventionality."[2] Sam Nash is, in fact, a conventional businessman who has made a successful life for himself. He has achieved the American dream: prosperity, marriage, and a family. Similarly, Karen Nash is a conventional 1950s-style wife, a homemaker whose entire focus during her twenty-three years of marriage has been on her husband and her two children. Yet neither Sam nor Karen is particularly happy. Sam is suffering from a midlife crisis and is terrified about growing old and flabby. "I don't have to accept being fifty-one," he tells his wife. "I don't accept getting older."[3] Karen, who is more concerned about the state of her marriage, is distressed that she and Sam have grown apart in recent months, even suspecting her husband of infidelity. Yet she is desperate to preserve her 1950s-style marriage—a bond that presumably invests the heroine with her only real sense of identity.

In "Visitor from Mamaroneck" Simon recycles the classic comedic theme of the battle of the sexes. As Richard P. Cooke writes, this first playlet depicts "one of those contests between the romantic practicality of womankind and the impractical romance of men."[4] Hoping to revive her marriage, Karen has deliberately arranged for the pair to celebrate their twenty-third anniversary by staying in the same hotel suite in which they spent their honeymoon. She has brought flowers to the room, as well as a sheer negligee, and has ordered champagne and hors d'oeuvres. Sam, however, who is currently enjoying an "impractical romance" with his young, attractive secretary, has absolutely no interest in reliving his honeymoon with Karen and indeed does everything in his power to sabotage his wife's romantic plans, even announcing that he must return to work at the office.

Although Karen and Sam eventually manage to suspend their battle and to communicate more openly with each other (he confesses his affair; she tries to forgive him), Simon does not provide his playlet with a happy ending and, in this sense, clearly deviates from the standard Menandrian plot. Unlike Corie and Paul Bratter in *Barefoot in the Park,* Karen and Sam do not reconcile with each other, nor do they revitalize their marriage. Instead, the battle of the sexes ends in a standoff. The audience does not know if Sam will return to Karen, if their marriage will survive, or even if she would be better off without her husband; and that is exactly the kind of open ending Simon wanted.

"Visitor from Hollywood"

Simon's second one-act play could well have been entitled "The Seduction." It describes an encounter at the Plaza Hotel between Jesse Kiplinger—a prominent Hollywood producer—and his former high-school girlfriend, Muriel Tate, whom he has not seen for the past seventeen years. "Visitor from Hollywood" adopts the basic Menandrian framework for a romantic comedy, particularly emphasizing the boy-wins-girl element of that well-known plot. But Simon's real subject is that of empty fantasies—and the banality of loveless relationships.

At first glance the play appears to describe the seduction of an innocent woman by a smooth-talking, cosmopolitan man. Jesse is pictured as a suave, forty-year-old celebrity who lives in the fast lane in Hollywood. Muriel, on the other hand, is described as a naive suburban housewife and mother who has never left her hometown in Tenafly, New Jersey. Yet both characters are not quite what they appear to be. Muriel eventually reveals (through her behavior as well as her conversation) that she is unhappily married, that she has a drinking problem, and that she is not the innocent teenager whom Jesse remembers. Similarly, Jesse discloses that success in Hollywood has failed to bring him personal happiness (he has suffered from three broken marriages) and that he is actually far less self-assured than his glamorous appearance would suggest.

As Robert K. Johnson has noted, "Visitor from Hollywood" focuses "not on the act of seduction, but on the motivations of the seducer and the seduced."[5] Muriel's primary reason for pursuing Jesse is that she is bored with her pedestrian life in the suburbs and is eager to be charmed by a Hollywood celebrity. Like a star-struck teenager, she calls him "Mr. Famous Hollywood Producer," claiming that if she had married Jesse instead of her husband, she would now be enjoying a glamorous life, "going to parties with James Garner and Otto Preminger, running around with the Rat Pack" (549). Jesse's chief reason for seducing Muriel, on the other hand, is that he actually dreams of escaping from Hollywood and returning to the innocent days of his youth. Tired of the phoniness and vacuity of the people who surround him in the movie industry, he tells Muriel that she is "the last, sweet, simple, unchanged, unspoiled woman living in the world today" (547). Just as Muriel has adopted a romanticized view of Jesse, so has he created an idealized image of her.

"Visitor from Hollywood" appears to end more happily than "Visitor from Mamaroneck," especially since it emphasizes the boy-wins-girl element of the standard Menandrian plot—Jesse's successful seduction of Muriel. The two characters ultimately get what they want the most: Muriel yearns to be romanced by a Hollywood celebrity, and Jesse wants to recapture his youth by making love to an innocent woman. Yet Simon's play differs from most romantic comedies in that there is an emptiness to this final union. As Robert K. Johnson observes, Jesse and Muriel are caught up in a daydream and essentially "fornicate a fantasy."[6] Muriel does not see Jesse for who he really is—a shallow, self-centered man who constantly needs to prove his masculinity through his sexual conquests; Jesse, likewise, ignores the fact that his high-school sweetheart has turned into a "middle-aged groupie. . . . a frustrated, calculating, hard-drinking housewife."[7] Beneath the comic surface of the play, therefore, lie more serious—and troubling—problems.

"Visitor from Forest Hills"

Simon labeled the final one-act play in *Plaza Suite* a farce; and indeed, like most farces, "Visitor from Forest Hills" presents a broadly humorous situation, relying chiefly on physical humor and exaggeration for its comic effect. The play presents a middle-aged couple, Norma and Roy Hubley, whose daughter has locked herself in the hotel bathroom on her wedding day, refusing to come out. As the wedding guests downstairs grow impatient, the Hubleys become increasingly frantic, eventually resorting to outrageous tactics in order to extricate their daughter from the bathroom. This final playlet focuses on the theme of lack of communication, especially between parent and child. But it also takes the traditional boy-wins-girl ending of Menandrian New Comedy (i.e., a wedding) and turns it into a near disaster.

The problem of communication between parent and child is made obvious by the play's farcical situation itself. Forced to speak to Mimsey through the bathroom door (a visible image of the communication barrier between them), Roy and Norma are unable to elicit a response from their daughter, who remains silent throughout most of the short drama. Rather than making an effort to understand Mimsey's wedding-day jitters, the parents are focused on their own concerns. Norma is fearful of the embarrassment that a canceled wedding will bring, while Roy is worried about the financial losses that he will suffer if the wedding actually fails to take place. After itemizing the vast sums of money he has already spent for food, liquor, and musicians, he yells, "Mimsey! This is your father. I want you and your four-hundred-dollar wedding dress out of there in five seconds!" (564).

Not only do Roy and Norma have problems communicating with their daughter but with each other as well. The Hubleys' marriage does not appear to be a happy one, and during this scene at the hotel the couple spend most of their time bickering and casting blame on each other. At the end of the play, we also learn the real reason for Mimsey's wedding-day panic: the girl is afraid of marriage because she is worried that she and her fiancé, Borden, will eventually become just like her parents. As Roy explains to Norma, their daughter "wants something better" (580).

"Visitor from Forest Hills" can be understood as an example of psychic farce, a form that Morton Gurewitch defines as follows: "Usually the protagonist of psychic farce oscillates unpredictably between reason and irrationality, maturity and infantilism, dignity and dishevelment—often simply by leaping from one emotion to its polar opposite. The essence of psychic farce, in short, is zany mental and emotional instability."[8] In Simon's playlet most of the hilarity is connected with Norma and Roy's frantic emotional state and their complete lack of control over the situation. Norma reveals her instability when she clutches her chest, claiming that she is having a heart attack; when she despairs over having ripped her stockings; and when she bangs so hard on the bathroom door that she breaks her diamond ring. Roy displays even more instability than his wife—hurling his body at the bathroom door, threatening to burn some newspapers and smoke his daughter out, and eventually crawling out on the ledge of their seventh-floor suite in order to enter the bathroom through the window.

In *The Play Goes On* Simon writes that a farce usually begins with a minor problem, which is compounded by a series of more complicated problems until calamity seems to threaten the characters. At the end, he says, "all the problems are solved in one hilarious sentence."[9] Such a description fits "Visitor from Forest Hills," which begins with the problem of Mimsey's wedding day jitters, expands

into the increasing problems encountered by her frantic parents—
nearly ruining the wedding—and concludes after Mimsey's fiancé,
Borden, using remarkably few words, successfully coaxes his bride
out of the bathroom. "Mimsey?" he says, "This is Borden . . . Cool
it!" (581). (In an updated version of the playlet in Simon's *Hotel
Suite* [2000], the fiancé simply says, "Chill out.")

Throughout *Plaza Suite* Simon declines to endorse the rosy
view of marriage that prevails in many comedies, including his own
lighthearted play *Barefoot in the Park.* Even in the farcical "Visitor
from Forest Hills," Roy wonders if his daughter should really marry
a man who communicates with words like "Cool it." He finally tells
Norma, "She was better off in the bathroom. You hear me? Better
off in the bathroom" (582). Given Simon's focus in *Plaza Suite* on
marital strife and the difficulties inherent in long-term relationships,
it is especially fitting that he would set these three plays in a hotel.
More than any other dwelling place, the hotel serves effectively as
an image of transience—of people who come and go, of casual intimacy, of impermanent human attachments. The Plaza Hotel itself
thus provides a symbolic backdrop for one of Simon's most significant themes: the human need for a love that is lasting.

Last of the Red Hot Lovers

When Simon wrote *Last of the Red Hot Lovers* (1969), he was in his
early forties and keenly aware of the sexual revolution that was taking place in America. "When did things change so fast?" he wondered. "I married at twenty-six, not exactly a man of the world but
still an idealistic youth looking for the perfect girl. And now, when
I was forty, they were dancing naked in a giant orchard in upstate

New York, and I was missing it."[10] Simon's restlessness and his brief impulse to separate from his first wife (an impulse that he never acted upon) became the inspiration for a comedy about the midlife crisis—a topic which Simon had already broached, to some extent, in *Plaza Suite.*

Presenting a more intricate variation of the ancient Menandrian plot, *Last of the Red Hot Lovers* adopts a "problem marriage" framework, as well as three different versions of the classical boy-meets-girl story. The plot for the play's three acts might be described as follows: act 1—boy meets girl, boy loses girl; act 2—boy meets girl, boy loses girl; act 3—boy meets girl, boy loses girl, boy wins wife. Notable for its affirmation of traditional values—particularly that of fidelity in marriage—the play describes the failed seduction attempts of Barney Cashman, a forty-seven-year-old restaurateur who fears that life is passing him by and who is strongly tempted to engage in an extra-marital affair. But during his separate encounters with three women (one in each act), Barney learns that he is not really destined for the role of "red hot lover" and that despite the sexual revolution going on around him, he cannot escape from his basic identity as a decent man.

Just as Sam Nash in *Plaza Suite* was afraid of aging, so is Barney Cashman. Indeed, Barney's midlife crisis has been precipitated by a powerful sense of his own mortality. He confides to Elaine Navazio (the first woman whom he attempts to seduce) that he is forty-seven years old and that for the first time in his life he is having thoughts about dying: "I read the obituaries every day just for the satisfaction of not seeing my name there."[11] Barney pictures himself as a devoted family man and upstanding citizen but someone to whom nothing extraordinary has ever happened. He runs a fish restaurant, enjoys a comfortable marriage with his wife, Thelma, and has raised three children. But he realizes that his life has become tediously routine, and he doesn't want to go to his grave feeling unfulfilled. Overwhelmed by ennui, Barney dreams of indulging in an illicit affair—of giving in to his secret fantasies at least once in his life.

Like the protagonists of most romantic comedies, Barney discovers that there are a number of obstacles to his success as a lover—one of them being his incongruous choice of setting for his amorous escapades: his mother's Manhattan apartment. Although Barney's mother never actually appears in the play, her presence looms over the apartment (especially in act 1), causing Barney to feel thoroughly inhibited in his role as Don Juan. He places his galoshes on a newspaper, not wanting to leave "telltale slush" (591) on the floor; he brings his own liquor and glasses instead of using his mother's; and he even forces himself to speak softly to Elaine, not wanting his mother's next-door neighbor to hear strange voices in the apartment. "Are you talking soft because you think that's sexier?" asks Elaine. "Because I don't find it sexy. I find it hard to hear" (591).

A more significant obstacle to Barney's success as a red-hot lover is his choice of prospective sexual partners. Elaine Navazio, in act 1, is perfectly willing to engage in an adulterous affair, but she makes it clear to Barney that she is simply satisfying certain physical cravings and has no interest in a romantic attachment. Bobbi Michele, in act 2, regales the protagonist with outlandish stories about her own sexual encounters, but she proves to be emotionally unbalanced and evinces no real attraction for Barney. And Jeanette Fisher, in act 3, is described not only as a friend of Barney's wife, Thelma, but as "probably the singularly most depressed woman on the face of the Western Hemisphere" (636). During the course of the play, Barney's choice of sexual partners thus becomes progressively worse: from Elaine, who is ready for sex but too aggressive; to Bobbi, who tells titillating stories but who is emotionally disturbed; to Jeanette, who is severely depressed and who appears to have no desire for sex at all.

Yet the biggest obstacle to Barney's success as a red-hot lover is Barney himself. A faithful husband for twenty-three years, the protagonist is pictured as conservative, overweight, and somewhat uncouth—the opposite of a slick ladies' man. Jeanette, in act 3, especially deals a blow to Barney's image as a modern-day Don Juan when she brings up the subject of obesity and announces that she is not physically attracted to him. The protagonist's old-fashioned romanticism also stands in the way of his success as a seducer. With Elaine, the first of his would-be conquests, Barney claims that he is not looking for a cheap affair but a fulfilling romantic experience, one that he will remember for the rest of his life. Elaine, however, who is simply interested in having sex, is not impressed by Barney's idealized view of romance and leaves the apartment declaring, "Good luck, Barney, in your quest for the Impossible Dream" (613).

Since Barney has chosen an inappropriate setting for these sexual liaisons, as well as a series of inappropriate partners, it can be argued that, at least subconsciously, he has been sabotaging from the start his efforts to break his marriage vows. Barney's misgivings about having an affair are suggested in act 1 when he admits to Elaine that he isn't being fair to his wife and that "if she indulged herself the same way I'd never forgive her" (612). These scruples are further revealed in act 3 when Barney tells Jeanette that it's not a good idea to test a marriage too much and that his wife, Thelma, is "the most decent human being on earth" (648). Finally, when Barney makes a desperate, crude advance to Jeanette, he is stopped in his tracks by her assertion that this behavior is totally out of character for him—that he, like Thelma, is at heart a "decent, gentle and loving" human being (646).

As David Grote points out, the "fading love" or "problem marriage" variation of the Menandrian plot normally concludes on a hopeful note: "There is no new marriage, since everyone is already married; however, the old marriage is renewed, made fresh and youthful again."[12] In keeping with this optimistic pattern, *Last of the Red Hot Lovers* closes with a renewal of Barney's marriage to Thelma. After Jeanette (the last of his would-be lovers) has departed, Barney places a call to his wife, inviting *her* to meet him at his mother's apartment. Thelma never actually appears onstage during the course of the play, nor does the audience hear her response to Barney's request. One can reasonably assume, however, that the protagonist's experience as a modern-day Don Juan is over. By extending this invitation to his wife, Barney reveals that he has learned the value of compromise and moderation. He recognizes, finally, that he does not necessarily need to be a red-hot lover in order to be himself.

In *Last of the Red Hot Lovers,* Simon makes use of a "pattern plot"—a format that Elder Olson defines as a series of actions, all of which involve the same situation. (For example, in Thornton Wilder's *The Queens of France* a man swindles three different women, each of whom he has deceived into thinking that she is the queen of France.)[13] In Simon's play the pattern plot unfortunately makes the second and third acts seem less witty and original than the first. Criticizing the repetitive structure, Walter Kerr wrote: "I suspect that it is time for Mr. Simon to put together a whole play again, with four and five and six people bumping into each other from time to time, and with the second and third acts standing on, instead of alongside, the first."[14] *Last of the Red Hot Lovers,* like *Plaza Suite,* gives the impression of being a group of one-act plays rather than a full-length drama.

But the pattern plot does have certain advantages. First, it allows the audience to compare the women whom Barney is pursuing and to appreciate their differing attitudes toward the sexual revolution—from Elaine, who is a willing participant in such a revolution; to Bobbi, who, at least in her imagination, has taken sexual liberation to an extreme; to Jeanette, who is totally repulsed by the sexual revolution and who no longer enjoys sex at all. The pattern plot also emphasizes the powerful nature of Barney's adulterous urge. As Paul H. Grawe notes, "The heavy-handed repetition suggests that modern man looks to sex as the only way out of boredom, that he will not give up after failure."[15] Furthermore, by repeating Barney's failures, the pattern plot helps to define Barney as a born loser, a stock figure in comedy with whom the audience can easily commiserate.

Most importantly, the pattern plot allows the audience to witness a certain amount of growth in Barney Cashman himself. Throughout much of the play Barney is pictured as an ill-intentioned fool—a naive and bumbling seducer. By the end of act 3, however, the protagonist appears to have learned from his repeated failures. He learns not only that his traditional values are central to his life but also that his urge to indulge in an affair—though improper—is not necessarily a sign of depravity. Near the end of *Last of the Red Hot Lovers,* Barney probably voices Simon's own tolerant view of humanity when he declares, "We're not indecent, we're not unloving. We're human. That's what we are, Jeanette, *human!*" (650).

Last of the Red Hot Lovers is ultimately a more optimistic drama than *Plaza Suite,* because it displays what Robert B. Heilman identifies as the hallmark of comedy: an attitude of acceptance. According to Heilman, comic acceptance is "a perception of the world as a livable middle ground that is not celestial but is not infernal either." It is an "accommodation to actuality." Heilman further argues that comic acceptance may include "acceptance of second best, that is, making do with something less than a total good that one is capable of imagining."[16] In *Last of the Red Hot Lovers* Barney Cashman, after his three botched attempts at seduction, clearly exemplifies such an attitude of comic acceptance, adjusting to a life that falls short of the ideal, and surviving, finally, by making do— by simply embracing the world as he knows it.

CHAPTER FIVE

The Gingerbread Lady and *The Prisoner of Second Avenue*

The Gingerbread Lady

After *Last of the Red Hot Lovers,* Simon took his playwriting in an even more serious direction, making an effort to combine tragedy with comedy in *The Gingerbread Lady* (1970) and *The Prisoner of Second Avenue* (1971)—two plays featuring middle-aged characters whose lives are spiraling out of control. Explaining the genesis of *The Gingerbread Lady,* Simon said: "I wanted to write a play about losers," about people "who have complete control over their own destiny, but who self-destruct because something moves them to make the wrong choices time and time again."[1] One of Simon's darkest dramas, *The Gingerbread Lady* examines the theme of self-destruction through its portrait of Evy Meara, an alcoholic ex-singer who cannot seem to put her life back together again. Like the little gingerbread lady in the window of her daughter's old gingerbread house, Evy is fragile and crumbles easily.

The question of whether tragic and comic elements should be mixed in drama has frequently been debated. During the Renaissance, Sir Philip Sidney denied the legitimacy of tragicomedy, whereas Samuel Johnson, in the eighteenth century, defended such a dramatic hybrid. Modern critics have generally been less inclined to view tragedy and comedy as polar opposites, admitting, as Elder Olson does, that "except for sheer slapstick and froth and buffoonery, there is always a serious element in comedy,"[2] or even arguing, as Northrop Frye does, that "tragedy is really implicit or uncompleted comedy," and "comedy contains a potential tragedy within itself."[3] For Simon, the desire to combine the tragic with the comic developed from his own life experience and from his role as a writer of realist drama. Although Lillian Hellman had earlier cautioned him not to blend tragedy with comedy, Simon himself was convinced that "if that can happen in life, why can't it happen in the theatre?"[4]

The tragic element of *The Gingerbread Lady* stems from Evy Meara's addiction to alcohol and from her overwhelming sense of personal failure. A former nightclub singer, the forty-three-year-old protagonist has ruined her own career and has no idea how she will support herself in the future. She has failed in her marriage (she and her husband have been divorced for seven years) as well as in her role as mother (her seventeen-year-old daughter, Polly, whom she hardly knows, has been raised by the girl's father and stepmother). As Michael Abbott suggests, Evy "is acutely aware of the scathing truth about herself: she is an unstable, self-obsessed, nymphomaniac alcoholic. She cannot sustain one meaningful relationship, not even with her own daughter."[5]

Like Tennessee Williams's character Blanche DuBois, Evy has sought escape from her problems not only through alcohol but also through sex, filling her life with casual intimacies. Evy's most recent lover, a guitar player named Lou Tanner, deserted the heroine for a much younger woman, causing Evy to go on a suicidal alcoholic binge before she entered the sanitarium. But the heroine is still both physically and emotionally dependent on Lou, resuming her relationship with him in act 2, even though the man is physically abusive. Suffering from a total lack of self-esteem, Evy, like a prototypical

battered woman, repeatedly involves herself with men who manipulate, wound, and discard her.

The protagonist's lack of self-worth is also illustrated by the
fact that she suffers from an apparent eating disorder. During her
ten-week stay at the sanitarium, Evy loses forty-two pounds and is
pleased by the reaction of her friends and daughter, who assure her
that she looks beautiful when she is "skinny and sober."[6] Yet three
weeks after her return from the sanitarium, Evy shows no real interest in food, subsisting instead on coffee and cigarettes. "I don't want
to take care of my body," Evy tells Polly. "I want somebody else
[i.e., a man] to take care of it" (184). But this joke cannot succeed in
masking Evy's self-destructive habits and her obvious lack of personal esteem.

Evy's downfall is caused not only by her own self-destructive
behavior but also by her lack of a positive support system. After her
release from the sanitarium Evy has no rehabilitation group in place
(like Alcoholics Anonymous) to help ease her transition back into
everyday life. Furthermore, she receives very little help from her
friends, who are as weak and dependent as she is and who basically
function as enablers in the heroine's prolonged battle with alcoholism. Jimmy Perry is a struggling gay actor who has tried to
take care of Evy in the past but who tends to confront her angrily
about her drinking—an approach that fails to promote her recovery.
Another of Evy's friends, Toby Landau, is a forty-year-old narcissist
who is so obsessed with her physical appearance that she has little time
to focus on Evy's problems. And the down-and-out musician, Lou
Tanner, is the most unsupportive friend of all, telling Evy, "In eight
weeks they might find you under the piano with a case of Thunderbird
wine. . . . Together, Evy, we don't add up to one strong person" (180).

The heroine's friends also function as enablers by drawing her into an atmosphere of crisis and disillusionment. Rather than helping Evy with her recovery, they are focused on their own emotional problems. Jimmy, who has been fired abruptly from the cast of a play in which he is performing, fears that he will never be able to find success as an actor. "Twenty-two years and I'm still expecting to get discovered" (192), he tearfully tells Evy. Similarly, Toby, who has just learned that her husband wants a divorce, is utterly devastated by the discovery that, at age forty, she is no longer as young and attractive as she used to be. Not only do Jimmy and Toby burden Evy with their personal problems, but they also drink openly in front of her—a behavior that unfortunately prompts the heroine to resume her destructive drinking habit.

Among this collection of losers, the one positive character is Evy's seventeen-year-old daughter, Polly, a selfless and devoted girl who has come to live with the heroine in order to assist in her mother's recovery. But during her turbulent stay with Evy, Polly herself proves to be an enabler; for she tries to control Evy—or to protect her from the consequences of her addiction—rather than placing the responsibility squarely on Evy's shoulders. Assuming the position of her mother's caretaker, Polly scolds Evy when she is late for dinner, chides her about her unhealthy lifestyle, and is appalled when she learns that her mother had a glass of sherry at Schrafft's. "*You've* got to take over, *you've* got to be the one in charge around here" (185), cries Polly, who is clearly uncomfortable with the current reversal of mother and daughter roles.

The basic situation in *The Gingerbread Lady* is a tragic one, to be sure; yet the dialogue itself is often amusing. Indeed, much of the humor in the play derives from Evy's caustic wit. No matter what the situation, the heroine is always ready with an amusing remark or barbed comment. According to Edythe M. McGovern, Evy lives "in a world where wisecracks serve to mask almost constant cries for help."[7] In other words, Simon connects the tragic and comic elements of his play by having his characters (especially Evy) employ humor as a defense mechanism.

Many of the heroine's facetious remarks are actually self-denigrating. Commenting on her lack of mothering skills, Evy says to Polly, "What kind of influence would I be on you? I talk filthy. I have always talked filthy. I'm a congenital filthy talker" (171). Later in the play she tells Polly that an eighty-six-year-old man with a cane flirted with her when she was out shopping. "I don't think he could see me or hear me too good but we really hit it off . . . If I don't get any better offers this week, I'm going to contact him at the Home" (182). Throughout the play Evy jokes about her nymphomania, about her alcoholism, about her inadequacies as a mother—all in an effort to minimize these problems. But she openly admits that she has "only one more chance at this human-being business . . . and if I blow it this time, they'll probably bury me in some distillery in Kentucky" (173).

Although a few critics, including Clive Barnes, spoke positively of Simon's attempt to combine tragedy and comedy in *The Gingerbread Lady,* many found the play deeply flawed. Martin Gottfried, for example, called it "trivial, plotless, characterless" and "a very leaky ship [which] has had its holes stuffed with jokes to keep it from sinking entirely."[8] Walter Kerr voiced a similar criticism, referring to the play as "a skeleton with bells on"—the bells being "a carillon of face-saving comebacks" that provoke our laughter. Evy, in particular, is not developed well as a character, Kerr argued. The audience never learns what her singing career was like or why she has chosen her particular group of friends. "She is a woman who drinks, and that is that."[9] Robert K. Johnson claimed that the characterization of Polly was also unconvincing—that she was "too good to be true" in her single-minded devotion to her mother.[10] And Stanley Kauffmann pointed out the implausibility of Polly's presence in Evy's home in the first place: "We are asked to believe that Evy's ex-husband sends their daughter to live with his nymphomaniacal ex-wife just out of an alcoholics' hospital."[11]

One of the most serious flaws in *The Gingerbread Lady* is its upbeat conclusion—an ending that was added after early runs of the play in New England. Simon originally wrote a somber ending in which Evy would argue with Polly, beg Lou to have sex with her again, and then, after getting drunk in the dark, submit to the advances of Manuel, the Puerto Rican grocery boy who first appeared at the beginning of act 1. When preliminary responses to the play were unfavorable, however, Simon decided to change his third act, creating a reconciliation between Evy and Polly and offering at least the hope that Evy might one day overcome her addiction. "When I grow up," Evy tells her daughter at the end of the revised version, "I want to be just like you" (227). Yet there is no reason to believe that Evy Meara will ever change, especially when she is surrounded by a group of enablers who unwittingly support her drinking. Although not a comic ending, the original conclusion to the play, in which Evy escapes once again in sex and alcohol, is much more realistic and appropriate than the revised version. Indeed, Simon himself ultimately regretted making the alteration. "I'm sorry I did [it]," he remarked. "I wish I had left it the other way."[12]

The Gingerbread Lady cannot be numbered among Simon's finer works; nevertheless, it is an important play in the author's dramatic canon, dealing with a darker subject than Simon had ever addressed before and introducing one of his most memorable female characters. Based on a number of actresses Simon had known over the years, Evy Meara reminded many theatergoers of the late Judy Garland—talented, charismatic, and poignantly self-destructive. Clive Barnes called Evy "a larger than life and yet still credible human being. A woman with incurable honesty and incurable weakness, who hides behind jokes that would make her a fortune as a jokewriter."[13] Humor is certainly the principal source of Evy's charm, but sadly enough, it is also her mask, her defense mechanism, and the only weapon the heroine seems to have left in her losing battle with alcoholism.

The Prisoner of Second Avenue

Simon's next dark comedy, *The Prisoner of Second Avenue* (1971), is noteworthy for its effort to engage in serious social commentary. Explaining the origins of this play, Simon remarked: "I was very down on New York at that point, which is about when the taxi drivers started putting up those barriers between themselves and their passengers. It seemed to me symptomatic of what was going on in all our cities: People were so alienated and so fearful that they were separating themselves from contact."[14] Focusing on urban angst and the midlife crisis of its protagonist, Mel Edison, *The Prisoner of Second Avenue* stands out in Simon's canon as one of his most iconoclastic works. Instead of validating traditional social norms, as he often does in his comedies, Simon offers a sharp critique of contemporary American society, picturing the urban experience, in particular, as a prison from which there is little hope of escape.

Like Barney Cashman in *Last of the Red Hot Lovers,* Mel Edison can be classified as a specific comedic type—the born loser (a type played to perfection by one of Simon's favorite movie comics, Charlie Chaplin). Like Barney, Mel feels frustrated and trapped, sensing, at age forty-seven, that his life is somehow slipping away from him. Yet Mel's situation is much bleaker than Barney's. In the first act of *The Prisoner of Second Avenue,* Mel is fired from the middle-level executive job that he has held for twenty-two years— a victim of corporate cutbacks. With two daughters in college, Mel is extremely anxious about his financial future and his ability to provide for his family. To make matters worse, he and his wife, Edna, are robbed during the first act of the play, the burglars taking many of their possessions, including the television, the liquor, Mel's suits, and the entire contents of the medicine cabinet.

Throughout the play Mel is overwhelmed by anxiety and despair, much in the manner of Willy Loman in Arthur Miller's *Death of a Salesman* (1949)—a drama that Simon called "maybe the best American play I've ever seen."[15] Although Mel is more comical and one-dimensional than Miller's protagonist, the two characters actually have a great deal in common. Both Willy and Mel find themselves trapped in a claustrophobic urban setting, boxed in by apartment buildings and other tall buildings. They complain about the overcrowding and the lack of fresh air. "There's not a breath of fresh air in the neighborhood," says Willy to his wife, Linda. "Smell the stink from that apartment house! And another one on the other side."[16] In Simon's play Mel Edison echoes Willy's sentiments when he tells Edna, "You can't breathe in here. . . . Christ, what a stink. Fourteen stories up, you can smell the garbage from here. . . . This country is being buried by its own garbage."[17] Like Willy, who dreams of getting a little place in the country where he can raise vegetables and chickens, Mel would undoubtedly be happier in a rural environment, far away from the modern urban problems that surround him. Edna's dream for her husband, in fact, is to have him run a summer camp for children in Vermont.

Overwhelmed by the pressures of urban life—the congestion, the crime, the threat of unemployment—Mel Edison, like Willy Loman, has begun to lose touch with reality. He complains loudly to Edna in the middle of the night about the terrible apartment that they live in—about the paper-thin walls, the air conditioner that doesn't function properly, and the toilet that doesn't stop flushing. Eventually he yells at his neighbors, banging on the walls and warning them to be quiet so that he can get some sleep. "I think I'm going out of my mind," he says to Edna. "I'm unraveling . . . I'm losing touch! . . . I don't know where I am half the time. I walk down Madison Avenue, I think I'm in a foreign country. . . . I don't know where or who I am any more. I'm disappearing, Edna" (238–39).

Depressed and paranoiac, Mel exemplifies what Elder Olson has termed comic suffering: "We find that scenes of comic suffering— fear where there is no cause for fear, anxiety where there is no cause for anxiety, embarrassment, desperation, absurd beatings, etc., are in fact among the funniest in comedy."[18] In Mel's case, there is actually some cause for anxiety, but his response to his predicament is exaggerated (e.g., he lashes out childishly at his neighbors and even insists that he is the victim of a vast, intricate plot to destroy the working classes of America). Furthermore, Mel's suffering itself often becomes a source of humor, as when he is doused by a bucket of water thrown by an irate upstairs neighbor. Pointing to the protagonist's many neuroses, Ellen Schiff calls Mel "a kvetching middle-aged Jew"[19] (though he is not explicitly identified as Jewish in the play); for Mel's brand of comic suffering is also consistent with a tradition of Jewish humor in which characters present themselves as beleaguered, self-pitying individuals—even martyrs. As Simon himself explained, it's an attitude of "everything happens to me."[20]

In order to emphasize that Mel's problems are shared by many city dwellers, Simon makes effective use of the device of a voice-over newscast. Just as the radio report in John Cheever's short story "The Enormous Radio" (1947) calls attention to broader tragedies outside the home of its protagonists, so does Simon's newscast accentuate the urban ills that beset many New Yorkers. In this case, however, the "bad news" is exaggerated to the point that it becomes comical. Roger Keating, the newscaster, reports on a robbery at the New York City Home for the Blind and a mugging of Governor Rockefeller; he warns that New York's water may be shut off the next day and encourages viewers to stay tuned for a filmed report "of how twenty million rats survive under the city" (273). In a subsequent newscast, we learn that Roger Keating himself was beaten and robbed outside the studio, that a Polish freighter crashed into the Statue of Liberty, and that a fierce winter storm is predicted to hit the eastern seaboard. According to Michael Woolf, such newscasts serve to portray the city "as an irrational landscape and the experience of the Edisons as more than personal misfortune. They are victims of a world close to a kind of absurd disintegration."[21]

Trapped in a hostile, urban environment, Mel does not face his problems in an adult manner but instead regresses into a state of childlike dependency. He broods, he wallows in self-pity, he blames everyone but himself, and he rejects the value of psychological counseling. Edna herself treats Mel like a child, coming home from work in the middle of the day in order to cook his lunch and suggesting that he amuse himself by playing softball with some of the boys from summer camp. Mel regards this mothering of him as an additional indignity, yet he makes no real effort to take charge of his life or to conduct himself in a responsible, adult manner. Mel's brother, Harry, who participates in a family conference about Mel's condition, is convinced that his brother is not a functioning adult. "I don't think you've got a brain for business," he tells Mel. "I don't think you know how to handle money. I don't think you can handle emotional problems. I think you're a child. A baby. A spoiled infant" (296).

Mel's child-like behavior is especially illustrated in his relationships with his neighbors in the apartment building. Not only does he bang on the wall when the flight attendants next door annoy him, but he also engages in shouting matches on the terrace with the neighbor above him, until the neighbor drenches him with a bucket of water. Vowing revenge, Mel buys a shovel with the intention of burying his neighbor in snow, planning to fling the snow down from a height of fourteen floors as his enemy approaches the building. Such a plan, of course, is simply another juvenile response on Mel's part—an irrational, childlike reaction to the pressures of urban life.

The Prisoner of Second Avenue concludes with a humorous tableau that suggests the grim survivor mentality of the Edisons. As a major snowstorm descends upon New York, Mel takes a shovel out of the closet and sits next to Edna on the sofa, with one arm around her shoulder, the other "holding the shovel upright at his side like a pitchfork"[22]—the two of them forming an image of Grant Wood's famous painting *American Gothic.* The image is effective not only because it is humorous but also because it suggests stasis and bleak realism: nothing will really change for city dwellers like the Edisons. In this final tableau, and in the play as a whole, Simon presents a dismal portrait of urban life, describing a city where people live like caged animals, alienated from other human beings; where crime, unemployment, noise, and overcrowding create an inordinate amount of stress, to the point that neighbors begin to battle with their neighbors. Indeed, in Simon's view, Mel's unseen neighbor upstairs symbolizes "a society gone mad, a world that was once civil, where people cared for people, but has now been reduced to a dog-eat-dog battlefield."[23] Unfortunately, Mel Edison, with his snow shovel poised for combat, remains part of this urban madness.

Reviewing *The Prisoner of Second Avenue* for the *New York Times,* Clive Barnes remarked on the increased seriousness of Simon's comedy: "Now his humor has a sad air to it; it is all the more deliciously funny for that undercurrent of discontent." According to Barnes, Simon had written a play about real human beings and real-life urban problems—crime, pollution, joblessness, and incivility—celebrating "our breast-beating comic agony in a gloriously funny play."[24] Although some critics found *The Prisoner of Second Avenue* weak in terms of plot and character development, the play did, at the very least, reflect Simon's continued interest in combining tragedy with comedy. Indeed, the term "serious comedy," though an oxymoron, seemed perfectly logical to the playwright himself.[25] As Barnes noted in his review, "Mel [Edison], prowling like a paper tiger in his paper house, is not merely a figure of fun. Mr. Simon understands the essential moroseness of comedy."[26]

CHAPTER SIX

The Sunshine Boys

Early in his career, when Simon was working as a comedy writer with his brother, Danny, he met an old vaudeville star named Willie Howard at New York's Astor Hotel. According to Simon, Willie was "a pint-sized man. . . . wearing a faded bathrobe over pajama tops, dark blue pants with suspenders, argyle socks, and a pair of slippers. I remembered seeing him when I was a young boy and how the tears ran down my cheeks at his preposterously funny routines." But now the aged vaudevillian was a picture of decline and a cheerless sight indeed: "The look and dress of Willie Howard, the seediness and sadness of his room, and the improbability that he would ever work much again stayed with me for years and finally became the model in my mind for what later would be *The Sunshine Boys*."[1]

Produced in 1972, *The Sunshine Boys* can be regarded as Simon's salute to vaudeville—his affectionate tribute to a bygone era of comedy. But the play is primarily centered on two themes: (1) old age—a subject that was new for Simon but one that he handled with sensitivity and skill; and (2) incompatibility—a theme that the playwright had previously explored in comedies such as *Barefoot in the Park* and *The Odd Couple*. Focusing on a pair of elderly comedians named Willie Clark and Al Lewis, *The Sunshine Boys* is an absorbing character study as well as one of Simon's most carefully structured comedies. Indeed, the play represented, in the author's view, "the best work I had done to date."[2]

Simon clearly believed that he was in his element when writing about vaudeville. As he later remarked, "I spent my life growing up with these men. If they spoke in one-liners and punch lines instead of conversation, it's because it was the only language they knew."[3] Not only was Simon able to experience vaudeville as a boy, but as an adult, he also absorbed its influence through the vaudeville-style sketches that were popular on radio and television. During the 1950s, in fact, Simon wrote a good number of those comedy sketches himself for television programs such as *The Garry Moore Show* and Sid Caesar's *Your Show of Shows.* Some of the basic staples of vaudeville humor—one-liners, gags, rapid-fire jokes, slapstick comedy—came easily, and quite naturally, to Simon.

As Bill Smith, author of *The Vaudevillians,* explains, vaudeville was a prime form of entertainment for Americans between 1880 and 1940, disappearing in the middle of the twentieth century after the advent of movies and television.[4] Essentially a variety show with assorted acts, vaudeville featured singers, dancers, acrobats, jugglers, magicians, dramatic actors, and comedians. Like New York's Broadway, Off-Broadway, and Off-off Broadway theater, vaudeville was divided into three main categories: big time, small time, and small-small time. Big-time vaudevillians, who were idolized like modern movie stars, usually performed two shows a day in the best theaters, enjoying good salaries and comfortable working conditions. Small-time and small-small-time vaudevillians, however, frequently worked four to six shows a day in modest venues and had to cope with inferior hotels and dressing rooms as well as with lower salaries. Although vaudeville performers could generally find steady work, they could not count on celebrity or financial success. Out of approximately ten thousand vaudevillians performing in America between 1920 and 1930, for example, only about eight hundred made the "big time."[5]

THE SUNSHINE BOYS

In *The Sunshine Boys,* Simon introduces two fictional characters who clearly made it to the "big time" in vaudeville. Based in part on the legendary vaudeville duo Smith and Dale, Al Lewis and Willie Clark once formed the famous comedy team of Lewis and Clark, or the Sunshine Boys. In the old days they worked in New York with stars like Sophie Tucker and were featured performers at the Palace—"the undisputed Tiffany's of show business."[6] Later, after the arrival of television, they appeared six times on *The Ed Sullivan Show*—the most popular variety show of the period. When the play begins, Lewis and Clark have been invited to participate in a CBS television special about the history of comedy— a program spotlighting some of the biggest names in show business. Willie's nephew, Ben Silverman, underscores the star quality of Lewis and Clark when he calls them "the two kings of comedy"[7] and "one of the greatest teams ever to come out of vaudeville" (315).

Unfortunately, the glory days of Lewis and Clark are far behind them. Not only has vaudeville itself become a forgotten art, but also Willie and Al are no longer a comedy team. The two men haven't even spoken to each other since Al's retirement eleven years ago, when Al abruptly broke up their partnership after a mediocre performance on *The Ed Sullivan Show*. Now Al lives quietly in New Jersey with his daughter's family, and Willie, though anxious to continue his show business career, has not had any real work for a long time. Simon also suggests the decline of vaudeville and its stars through his description of the play's main setting. Probably recalling his visit with real-life vaudevillian Willie Howard, Simon reveals that Willie Clark lives in a shabby two-room suite in an old Broadway hotel—his previous large suite now divided up into five minuscule apartments. The furniture is cheap, the radiator doesn't work, and the entire hotel is in a state of disrepair.

Simon's real theme, however, is not the demise of vaudeville but the aging process itself. In earlier comedies like *Plaza Suite* and *Last of the Red Hot Lovers,* the author explored the impact of the aging process on middle-aged men, but this is the first play in which he addresses the subject of old age. As usual, Simon approaches his topic with a mixture of humor and pathos. Willie Clark, now in his seventies, is portrayed as having a number of age-related problems. He is often confused and forgetful, mistaking the sound of a teakettle for his telephone at the start of the play or inadvertently pulling out his television cord and thinking that the set is broken. When Ben arrives for his weekly visit, Willie doesn't seem to know what day it is; he can't recall the names of Ben's children. Worse yet, his faulty memory is affecting his prospects for an acting job, because he can't remember the lines anymore.

Willie also finds that as an elderly man he must struggle for self-respect and independence. When he telephones downstairs to complain about his television set not working, he instructs the hotel employee not to call him Willie, but "Mr. Clark." Similarly, he balks at some of Ben's efforts to take care of him, not wanting to be overly dependent on his nephew. He tells Ben that he has never asked him for anything—except a job. "You're a good boy," he remarks, "but a stinking agent" (316). It is the job, in fact, that Willie needs the most, not so much for financial reasons but for the self-esteem that it will provide him. Willie is an actor, a comedian, a performer—someone for whom show business is everything. Even though his best days are behind him, he is simply not ready to be retired.

THE SUNSHINE BOYS

Unlike Willie, Al Lewis appears to have accepted his old age gracefully. About seventy years old, Al suffers from asthma, arthritis, and poor blood circulation. In addition, he is said to have diabetes, bad vision, and hardening of the arteries. But his mind is sharp, and he spends no time bemoaning his current situation. Since the death of his wife two years ago, Al has lived in New Jersey with his daughter's family, leading a very serene existence. In contrast to Willie, Al does not appear to need a show business career in order to be content. He even tells Ben, "it's not my New York [any more]" (329), as if to acknowledge his separation from the show business world, as well as the inevitability of aging.

The Sunshine Boys deals not only with the problems of the elderly but also with the difficulties that their caregivers experience. As Willie's only living relative, Ben is shouldering a considerable burden. He is worried about his uncle's health—afraid that Willie is not eating properly, that his blood pressure is too high, and that he is not obeying his doctor's order to give up cigars. Furthermore, Ben is increasingly concerned that Willie may no longer be capable of living independently. After Willie suffers a heart attack in act 2, Ben must help his uncle adjust to the idea of retiring permanently from show business and moving into the Actors' Home in New Jersey. Ben must also deal with Willie's continued antipathy toward his partner, Al Lewis—a circumstance that raises Willie's blood pressure and puts him at risk for another heart attack. Arranging for Al to visit his recuperating uncle, Ben understands that Willie can only be emotionally healthy again by making peace with his former partner.

A vaudeville team for forty-three years, Lewis and Clark, or the Sunshine Boys, were pioneers in the field of comedy; yet there was actually very little sunshine in their personal relationship. The two men never really got along with each other and in many ways represented an "odd couple." According to Willie, Al would deliberately torment him on stage—"giving him the finger" by poking him in the chest to make a point or spitting at him when he said words beginning with the letter "T." Willie is especially angry that Al suddenly retired eleven years earlier, breaking up their famous comedy team and leaving Willie to fend for himself. So resentful is he that he deliberately sabotages the two men's first rehearsal for the CBS television special, provoking an argument and even threatening Al with a knife.

Despite their incompatibility, however, Willie and Al have always had a close, symbiotic relationship.[8] When Ben asks Willie why he remained partners for forty-three years with a man he despised, Willie explains that there was no better comedian than Al and that he and Al somehow made a perfect professional team. "Nobody could time a joke the way he could time a joke," says Willie. "Nobody could say a line the way he said it. I knew what he was thinking, he knew what I was thinking. One person, that's what we were" (319). This symbiotic relationship is accentuated in act 2, when the television announcer introduces Lewis and Clark as "two comic shining lights that beam as one. For, Lewis without Clark is like laughter without joy" (353). Such a close relationship eventually creates a major problem for Willie, however, because throughout his career his identity has been inextricably linked with that of Al Lewis; without Al, there somehow is no Willie Clark any more.

In act 2 of his comedy Simon makes use of the ancient device of the play-within-the-play in order to bring the vaudeville of the Sunshine Boys to life again. He presents the sketch "The Doctor and the Tax Examination," an act that was probably modeled on the famous Dr. Kronkite routine of real-life vaudevillians Smith and Dale.[9] Set at a CBS television studio, the play-within-the-play reunites Willie and Al professionally, demonstrating—at least temporarily—how expertly they once functioned as a comedy team. During the sketch Willie (the doctor) and Al (the tax collector) are examining each other simultaneously, using a series of wisecracks such as the following:

Willie   I went to Columbia Medical School.

Al   Did you pass?

Willie   Certainly.

Al   Well, you should have gone *in*!

Willie   Never mind . . . I'm gonna examine your eyes now.

Al   They're perfect. I got twenty-twenty eyes.

Willie   That's too much. All you need is one and one.

(359)

Besides spotlighting the comedic talent of Lewis and Clark, the play-within-the-play underscores the enormous influence of vaudeville on the two men's personal lives. According to Robert K. Johnson, "The skit is more than good fun; it dramatizes in a thoroughly delightful way just how completely such sketches came to dominate the way both Willie Clark and Al Lewis thought and spoke every day of their lives."[10] Indeed, the language of vaudeville—especially the use of snappy one-liners—permeates the everyday speech patterns of Lewis and Clark. As critic Edwin Wilson observes, the lines in the doctor sketch "are not too different from many in the play itself."[11] Consider the vaudevillian flavor of this early exchange between Willie and Al, after Al has announced that his health is perfect:

Willie   I heard different. I heard your blood didn't circulate.

Al   Not true. My blood circulates . . . I'm not saying *everywhere,* but it circulates.

Willie   Is that why you use the cane?

Al   It's not a cane. It's a walking stick . . . Maybe once in a great while it's a cane.

Willie   I've been lucky, thank God. I'm in the pink.

Al   I was looking. For a minute I thought you were having a flush.

(334)

Vaudevillian gags (like Willie's inability to unlock his front door) are also integrated smoothly into *The Sunshine Boys,* accentuating the idea that Willie is growing old and that such problems are now part of his daily experience. Indeed, by mingling vaudevillian features of the doctor sketch with the rest of the play, Simon emphasizes that Lewis and Clark are in some ways still living their lives as an extended comedy routine.

The play-within-the-play is never completed, largely because Willie sabotages the filming of the vaudeville sketch, just as he sabotaged the earlier rehearsal in his apartment. Although Al is partly to blame for the two men's bitter argument (he deliberately pokes Willie in the chest again), it is Willie who provokes his partner by stubbornly uttering the word "Enter" instead of "Come in." In essence, Willie is changing the vaudeville act, compromising the integrity of a routine that was very special—and perhaps almost sacred—to Al. As Bill Smith points out, "the act was everything to the vaudevillian. Into it he poured all his knowledge, hard work, skill, time, and money." Each act was carefully practiced, and experienced vaudevillians knew their routines perfectly. Consummate professionals on stage, "they brooked no nonsense or interference"[12] as they practiced their highly disciplined art. Willie's use of the word "Enter" definitely constituted "nonsense" and "interference" in Al's mind; and the doctor sketch, as Al saw it, was irreparably ruined from the start.

Like most comedies, *The Sunshine Boys* moves toward a final sense of reconciliation and harmony. The first reconciliation takes place between Willie and Ben when they discuss Willie's future living situation and the advantages of retiring to the Actors' Home in New Jersey. Assuring Willie that he will be there every week for a visit, Ben adds, "You know, this is the first moment since I've known you, that you've treated me like a nephew and not an agent. It's like a whole new relationship" (379). Simon doesn't allow the reconciliation between Ben and Willie to become overly sentimental, however; for Willie dryly remarks, "I hope this [relationship] works out better than the other one," and he warns, "If you kiss me, I call off the whole thing" (379).

A more important reconciliation—or truce, if you will—occurs between the Sunshine Boys themselves at the end of the play. After the two men agree that their incessant arguments tend to tire them out, they lapse into milder conversation and the vaudeville-style repartee that both men enjoy. Even when Al reveals that he, too, will soon be moving into the Actors' Home in New Jersey, Willie accepts the shocking news with resignation. The play closes with an image of the two old comedians together again, reminiscing about old times and arguing good-naturedly about the names of people from their vaudeville past. Unlike *The Odd Couple,* in which Simon sacrificed consistency of character for the sake of a happy ending,

The Sunshine Boys concludes with a suggestion of harmony but with an emphasis on the continued rivalry between Lewis and Clark. Simon thus manages to be true to his comic genre but at the same time to accede to the demands of realism, offering an ending that is not only plausible but that is also perfectly in character for his two aged vaudevillians.

Most critics agree that *The Sunshine Boys,* though highly amusing, has an unmistakably sad air to it. Martin Gottfried calls the play "a melancholy valentine to American vaudeville," describing Willie Clark as "the representative of a wonderful, obsolete American tradition."[13] Other critics view the play, as Simon himself did, as a serious comedy about old age. Edythe M. McGovern, for instance, claims that despite the comic ending to the play, "there is a pervasive sense of desperation here too, not because we must all experience a 'final curtain' at the end of our play, but because so often there is no applause for actors who do not have the grace to quit the stage before they have grown old."[14] In a recent analysis of *The Sunshine Boys,* Ruby Cohn notes that Simon leaves us with the melancholy image of two old men rambling on about the past—"a preview of twilight in the Actors' Home." Furthermore, she argues that Simon's picture of old age is distinctly unsentimental: "Out of the public eye, old age is dramatized as dirty, demeaning, confusing, and utterly lonely. Yet Simon also makes it funny, so that we laugh with a sympathy that the selfish old souls scarcely deserve."[15]

The melancholy tone of *The Sunshine Boys* can be explained not only by Simon's basic outlook on life ("My view is 'how sad and funny life is'")[16] but also by his personal circumstances at the time that the play was written. In the fall of 1971 Simon's thirty-eight-year-old wife, Joan, was diagnosed with breast cancer. The doctors informed Simon that she had only about eighteen months to live. When the playwright received this devastating news, he had been working on *The Sunshine Boys* and had completed a first draft. Hoping to lift his own spirits and to restore some sense of normality to their lives, he eventually returned daily to the writing of the play. "The work was my refuge," he explained.[17] In July 1973, less than seven months after the opening of *The Sunshine Boys,* Joan Simon died. Because the play was completed during her prolonged illness, it is little wonder that this comedy about two old vaudevillians would prove to be a "melancholy valentine"—touched with nostalgia and with sadness.

CHAPTER SEVEN

California Suite

In the early seventies Simon experimented with several new dramatic forms, writing *The Good Doctor* (1973)—a series of sketches based on short stories by Chekhov—and *God's Favorite* (1974), an adaptation of the Biblical story of Job. With *California Suite* (1976), however, Simon returned to the successful format he had employed in *Plaza Suite,* presenting a group of one-act plays that are set in the same suite of the Beverly Hills Hotel. Although *California Suite* lacks the overall unity of *Plaza Suite,* the four sketches are connected by their satiric attacks on West Coast culture and by one of Simon's most prevalent themes: the need for reconciliation.

James Joyce once referred caustically to the one-act play as "dwarf drama,"[1] but throughout his career Simon has frequently been drawn to this dramatic form. Not only do *Plaza Suite, California Suite,* and the more recent *London Suite* (1995) consist of a group of one-act plays, but works such as *Last of the Red Hot Lovers* and *The Good Doctor* can also be placed in this category. Simon's early training as a comedy writer for television (where variety sketches and situation comedies were essentially playlets) undoubtedly inclined him toward this form of drama, but it was the spareness and intensity of the genre that especially appealed to him. As Simon once explained, with a one-act play "you can get straight to the big scenes, the crucial moments, the immediate laughs."[2] This is precisely what he manages to do in *California Suite.*

"Visitor from New York"

Simon begins his group of plays with a rather serious drama about the issue of child custody. Divorced for nine years, Hannah and Bill Warren meet at the Beverly Hills Hotel to debate future living arrangements for their seventeen-year-old daughter, Jenny. Although Hannah shares an apartment in New York with her daughter and has legal custody of her, the girl now wishes to remain in Los Angeles with her father. A variation of the Menandrian "problem marriage" plot, "Visitor from New York" makes use of the age-old comedic subject of the battle of the sexes. But it also explores the theme of the parent-child bond, affirming the characters' need, even after a divorce, for some semblance of family unity.

By the time *California Suite* was produced, Simon had married his second wife, actress Marsha Mason, and had moved to Southern California. Yet as Clive Barnes noted in his review of the play, "Although Mr. Simon has gone west, to become what is sometimes known as a Californian, his heart is still Manhattan, very dry and on the rocks."[3] Indeed, in *Rewrites* Simon tells of his apprehensions about working in Los Angeles early in his career, admitting to his East Coast prejudices: "I'm not sure why we diehard New Yorkers looked down our noses at Los Angeles, even knocking their health-food style as something to be avoided at all costs, while we gorged ourselves on sandwiches piled high with fats and named after comedians like Henny Youngman or Milton Berle."[4] Simon could thus identify with Hannah Warren, the diehard New Yorker who is eager to criticize every aspect of Southern California life, but he could also empathize with her ex-husband, Bill, the transplanted New Yorker and screenwriter who is seeking to make a new life for himself in the West.

As Edythe M. McGovern writes, the humor in this first playlet "depends almost entirely on the traditional rivalry which exists between New Yorkers and Angelenos, particularly the transplanted variety."[5] Hannah, who is an editor for *Newsweek,* makes fun of the California weather (where there will be no snow for Thanksgiving), of Bill's suntan ("You have an office outdoors somewhere?")[6], of her ex-husband's new, healthy lifestyle (which includes a vegetarian diet, exercise, and no psychoanalyst), and of the shallow materialism that pervades Southern California. She wonders what her daughter is going to learn "in a community that has valet parking just to pick up four bagels and the *Hollywood Reporter*" (561). Bill in turn accuses Hannah of East Coast snobbery and oversophistication, arguing that New York City is not the center of the universe and claiming that he wouldn't want to endure "another intellectual Cape Cod summer . . . The political élite queuing up in old beach sandals to see Bogart pictures, standing there eating ice cream cones and reading the *New Republic*" (561). These East Coast/West Coast attacks are merely opening salvos, however, in the couple's real battle over the custody of their daughter.

Simon's portrait of Hannah suggests not only the author's bias against East Coast sophistication but also his underlying distrust of the women's movement. Unlike the female characters in Simon's earlier plays, who tended to be conventional housewives and mothers, Hannah Warren is pictured as a liberated woman of the seventies whose work as a *Newsweek* editor is central to her life. "For a smart lady in a man's world, I'm not doing too bad" (568), she boasts. But the professional success made possible by the women's movement has brought Hannah neither happiness nor emotional security. Her lover from the *Washington Post* does not have long to live; she was forced to have a hysterectomy and is afraid of getting older; she sees an analyst three times a week; and she worries that she has not been a particularly good mother to Jenny. Trying to live up to the demands of what Betty Friedan called "the feminine mystique," Hannah has discovered that it is virtually impossible to find that elusive balance between motherhood and career.

Just as the women's movement has failed to bring happiness to Hannah, so have bachelorhood and commercial success failed to provide Bill with a sense of personal stability. Forty-five years old and twice divorced, with a history of emotional problems, Bill realizes that there is something important missing in his life: a sense of roots and family. He is currently involved in a serious relationship with an actress whom he hopes to marry. "Strange as it seems," he confides to Hannah, "I like being married" (559). But recognizing that he is growing older, Bill is also eager for one last opportunity to be a full-time father to Jenny before his daughter is completely grown up. It is his role as father, rather than his work as a Hollywood screenwriter, that gives him a feeling of purpose and belonging.

In "Visitor from New York," the "problem marriage" plot does not end, as it does in *Barefoot in the Park* or *Last of the Red Hot Lovers,* with a renewal of the protagonists' marriage but instead with a reaffirmation of their shared love for their daughter. Bill and Hannah manage to arrive at a tentative agreement about Jenny, who will remain with her father in California for the next six months. Signaling her truce with Bill with a handshake, Hannah adds tearfully, "I suddenly feel like an artist selling a painting he doesn't want to part with"—to which Bill responds gently, "I'll frame it and keep it in a good light" (572).

Although the battle of the sexes in this playlet thus concludes on a note of harmony, the characters themselves cannot be regarded as happy or serene. Hannah is pained by the loss, however temporary, of her only child, and Bill is distinctly anxious about the prospect of full-time fatherhood. Throughout their encounter Hannah and Bill have attempted to hide behind masks of witty sophistication, but, as Edythe M. McGovern notes, "one feels that beneath these disguises both Hannah and Bill have faces deeply etched by pain, faces which neither dares uncover too often, even when only looking into a mirror."[7] Despite the clever repartee of this sketch, therefore, it is by no means a traditional comedy.

"Visitor from Philadelphia"

In the second sketch Simon shifts from the serious tone of "Visitor from New York" and offers a bedroom farce in the style of Georges Feydeau, the master of French comic theater at the turn of the century. Simon again makes use of the Menandrian "problem marriage" plot, focusing on the issue of infidelity and concluding his sketch, as Feydeau does in *A Flea in Her Ear* (1907), with a revitalization of the protagonist's marriage.

Like most farces, "Visitor from Philadelphia" is based on a wildly improbable initial situation. Nursing a hangover, forty-two-year-old Marvin Michaels awakens in his hotel suite to find an intoxicated prostitute in his bed (a gift from his brother, Harry, the previous evening). Shocked to learn that his wife, Millie, is on her way up to the room, Marvin must somehow hide the unconscious body of the call girl from his wife. This outrageous situation resembles that in Feydeau's farce *La Dame de Chez Maxim* (1899), in which the protagonist, Petypon, hung over from his previous night's escapades, must conceal from his wife the cabaret singer whom he has just discovered in his bed. In Simon's playlet, Marvin quickly covers the prostitute with blankets and tries frantically to prevent his wife from entering the bedroom. The unconscious form of the woman, who is onstage throughout the performance, thus provides a key visual gag that accounts for much of the play's hilarity.

Like Feydeau's character, Simon's protagonist resorts to absurd diversion tactics during the frantic attempt to conceal his adultery. In *La Dame de Chez Maxim,* Petypon claims that he is having an attack of "hangovitus" and begs his wife to hold him tightly and turn him toward the north—away from the concealed cabaret singer: "No, no! Not that way, that's the south . . . In attacks like this you always turn the patient toward the north."[8] Similarly, in "Visitor from Philadelphia," Marvin informs Millie that he is suffering from acute gastroenteritis after eating spaghetti with tacos and some "tortillas parmegan" at a Mexican-Italian restaurant. Desperately trying to keep his wife out of the bedroom, Marvin even suggests that the two of them make love on the living room rug—to which Millie responds, "That's not a rug. It's carpeting. I don't like to make love on carpeting" (584).

Marvin resembles Barney Cashman in *Last of the Red Hot Lovers* in that he is a basically decent man who is devoted to his wife and children. Indeed, the protagonist assures Millie that during their fifteen-year marriage he has never even looked at another woman. Neither promiscuous nor uncaring, Marvin is simply an ordinary man overcome by a moment of weakness. He admits that he was intoxicated the previous evening and that he wasn't prepared to deal rationally with the "gift" that his brother, Harry, sent to his hotel room. "I never expected anything like this—I thought maybe a basket of fruit" (588). More important, Marvin is sincerely repentant about his actions, telling his wife, "It will never happen again because not only did I not enjoy it, I don't even remember it" (589).

Like a classical Menandrian comedy, the sketch moves toward a reconciliation between Marvin and Millie and a renewal of their fifteen-year marriage. The reconciliation is achieved by Marvin's confession of adultery (including the revelation of the inert form of the prostitute), by his desperate plea for forgiveness, and by Millie's eventual willingness to give their marriage another chance. Simon adds a touch of realism to this ending, however, by accentuating the wife's emotional pain. Not only does Millie cry when speaking to her children on the telephone, but she also makes it clear to Marvin that this reconciliation will inevitably have its price: "I am now going into Beverly Hills," she tells him, "and spend every cent you've got" (590).

In *The Life of the Drama* Eric Bentley argues that farce offers theatergoers a form of wish fulfillment—a kind of comic catharsis: "Shielded by delicious darkness and seated in warm security, we enjoy the privilege of being totally passive while on stage our most treasured unmentionable wishes are fulfilled before our eyes. . . . In that application of the formula which is bedroom farce, we savor the adventure of adultery, ingeniously exaggerated in the highest degree, and all without taking the responsibility or suffering the guilt."[9] "Visitor from Philadelphia" may indeed provide the audience with the fulfillment of repressed wishes. After all, Marvin Michaels does commit adultery (with an attractive call girl named Bunny, no less), and he does so with relative impunity. The audience is allowed to participate vicariously in this bizarre adventure, laughing at Marvin's ludicrous efforts to conceal his wrongdoing but suffering none of the protagonist's guilt.

According to Bentley, bedroom farce typically belittles the institution of marriage—seeking "to damage the family, to desecrate the household gods. . . . Outrage to family piety and propriety is certainly at the heart of farce."[10] But such an attack is clearly minimized in Simon's playlet. By the end of "Visitor from Philadelphia," when Marvin and Millie manage to reconcile, Simon suggests that marriage is still a valuable institution and, in the long run, something worth saving. "I would like to make a fresh start," says Millie. "I would like to try and rebuild our marriage on trust and faith" (590). This playlet resembles, in fact, some of Feydeau's best known farces in which, as Morton Gurewitch notes, "adulterous urges are also ultimately tethered, if not dashed, by bourgeois propriety." Like Feydeau's comedies, Simon's sketch essentially "plays with fire" but, in the end, "provides its own fire extinguisher."[11]

"Visitors from London"

The most successful of the four playlets in *California Suite,* "Visitors from London" is essentially a high comedy in the style of Noël Coward. Aiming for seriousness and sophisticated wit, Simon depicts the complex relationship between a middle-aged British couple, Diana and Sidney Nichols, who are visiting Los Angeles in order to attend the Academy Awards ceremony. In scene 1 the playlet focuses on the prelude to the Academy Awards, when Diana is extremely nervous about appearing on national television as a nominee for best actress; in scene 2 it focuses on the aftermath of the ceremony, when she is upset not only by her failure to win an Oscar but also by her troubled relationship with her husband. As in the two previous sketches, Simon makes use of the Menandrian "problem

marriage" framework, emphasizing at the end of the playlet the
characters' need for mutual understanding and for some kind of loving reconciliation.

An important feature of high comedy that is evident in "Visitors
from London" is the use of witty repartee by characters who are
socially sophisticated. Dressing for the Oscars ceremony, for
instance, the elegant Diana claims that her evening gown is bunched
up oddly on her left shoulder, making her resemble Richard III:

Diana	Do you notice the hump, Sidney?
Sidney	Isn't that your regular hump?
Diana	Don't joke with me. I'm going on national television.
Sidney	There are no humps. I see no humps at this particular time. . . . Have you taken out all the tissue paper?
Diana	I should have worn something simple . . . My black pants suit. Why the hell didn't I wear my black pants suit?
Sidney	Because *I'm* wearing it.

(593)

Simon was pleased by his success in bringing these English characters to life, particularly his ability to make their sophisticated banter
and their British dialogue sound genuine. Indeed, the humor of the
sketch derives almost exclusively from what the two characters say
rather than what they do.

Another feature of high comedy found in "Visitors from London"
is the play's satirical tone—specifically its ridicule of West Coast
manners and its attack on the artificiality and crassness of Hollywood.

In scene 2, when Diana and Sidney return from the Academy Awards after Diana has failed to win the Oscar, Sidney complains about the hypocrisy of everyone in the movie industry. "They all love you and fawn over you on the way in. And if you come out a loser, it's 'Too bad, darling. Give us a call when you're back in town' . . . You should have thrown up on the whole bloody lot of them" (606). Diana reflects on how the Hollywood crowd is too uncultivated to appreciate her illustrious dramatic career in England, where she performed in plays by some of the world's greatest dramatists. "I finally get nominated for a nauseating little comedy" (596), she laments. "That's why they call it Hollywood" (596), answers Sidney, who also mentions that Jack Nicholson wore black patent leather tennis shoes to the Academy Awards and that "they're not civilized out here, it's as plain as that" (608).

Like most high comedies, Simon's playlet offers a serious character study, accentuating the human side of Diana and Sidney Nichols. Throughout the playlet Simon pictures Diana as an accomplished actress but an emotionally insecure woman. She is extremely nervous about participating in the Academy Awards ceremony, dreading the thought of losing to someone like Faye Dunaway. Her concern about her appearance—her hair, her dress, and especially the "hump" on her shoulder—likewise reflects her self-consciousness and her general lack of self-esteem. In scene 2, when Diana returns from the Academy Awards without the coveted Oscar, she looks into the mirror and bemoans the fact that she is getting older. "I've aged, Sidney," she says. "I'm getting lines in my face . . . I look like a brand new steel-belted radial tire" (607).

Diana's insecurity (especially her fear that she is no longer an attractive woman) becomes perfectly understandable when the audience learns in scene 2 that Sidney is bisexual and that he has come to California, in part, in order to make new sexual contacts. Angered that her husband flirted with a handsome young actor at the Academy Awards ceremony, an intoxicated Diana proceeds to attack her husband openly for his infidelity, cruelly referring to him at one point as a "faggot." In his previous comedies that employed the Menandrian "problem marriage" framework, Simon had dealt with the issue of infidelity, but "Visitors from London" is his first play in which the central obstacle to a happy marriage is actually the sexual orientation of one of the characters.

Although Sidney's bisexuality is not openly revealed until scene 2, it is subtly suggested earlier in the play. Diana recalls that as an actor, Sidney had a "sweet, gentle quality" (599) on the stage and agrees that he would have been an excellent Ophelia. Sidney even jokes that he could not return to the theater now, because he and Diana would be competing for the same roles. Expressing his gratitude to Diana for putting up with his "shenanigans" for the last twelve years, Sidney admits at the end of scene 1 that she essentially has been left with "half a husband" (600).

According to Richard Grayson in "'The Fruit Brigade': Neil Simon's Gay Characters," homosexual figures are generally presented in a sympathetic light in Simon's comedies, although they are "somewhat pathetic."[12] Simon's first gay character, the washed-up actor Jimmy Perry in *The Gingerbread Lady* (1970), is basically portrayed as a weak individual, despite being a compassionate friend to the play's alcoholic heroine, Evy Meara. Sidney Nichols, however, is pictured as a more complex human being, with admirable qualities such as wit, refinement, and sensitivity. Indeed, as Robert K.

Johnson suggests, it is Diana, rather than Sidney, who is superficial and self-centered. "She knows . . . that even though the world at large idolizes her and would condemn Sidney for his homosexuality, nevertheless, Sidney is a finer, more admirable person than she is."[13]

It should be noted that almost twenty years after the production of *California Suite,* Simon wrote a sequel to "Visitors from London"—the "Diana and Sidney" playlet in *London Suite* (1995), depicting homosexuality (or bisexuality) as less of an aberration and also dealing with the difficult subject of AIDS. As Grayson argues, Simon's plays thus reflect the social changes that have taken place within this country over the last few decades, and "the evolution of his thinking about homosexuality since the 1970s approximates the earnest, well-meaning tolerance of his audiences."[14]

Toward the end of "Visitors from London," Diana and Sydney make an effort at reconciliation, as did Hannah and Bill Warren in "Visitor from New York" and Millie and Marvin Michaels in "Visitor from Philadelphia." When Diana wonders aloud why she and her husband continue to stay together, Sidney answers, "Because we like each other . . . And we are each a refuge for our disappointments out there" (613). In short, Diana and Sidney are friends, they take care of each other, and they know each other completely. As Sidney says, "I've never stopped loving you . . . in my way" (611). But the renewal of the couple's marriage (the typical end to the Menandrian plot) is undercut by Diana's continued insecurity and by Sidney's guilt about being "half a husband" to his wife. When the couple begin to make love at the end of the play, Diana begs Sidney not to close his eyes and dream of someone else: "Not tonight . . . Look at *me* tonight . . . Let it be *me* tonight" (614). Simon leaves little doubt, therefore, that this marriage between a love-starved actress and her bisexual husband still rests on extremely shaky ground.

"Visitors from Chicago"

The final playlet is a psychic farce that derives its humor from the irrational behavior of its characters. Unlike the three previous sketches, "Visitors from Chicago" focuses not on marital problems or infidelity but on the strained friendship between two couples, Mort and Beth Hollender and Stu and Gert Franklyn. The four characters have been vacationing together for the past few weeks, but they have begun to get on each other's nerves. A series of accidents occurs, tempers flare, and suddenly the suite at the Beverly Hills Hotel turns into a combat zone. As in other plays, Simon highlights the difficulty of maintaining long-term relationships, affirming in this sketch that familiarity indeed breeds contempt, even among the best of friends.

The reasons for the friction between the two couples are seemingly petty. Mort criticizes Stu and Gert for not traveling light, wondering why a skinny pair like them are lugging around eight pieces of luggage. Stu resents the fact that in Honolulu Mort and Beth enjoyed a room with a view, while he and Gert were compelled to share a room with a broken toilet. He is also tired of the smell of Mort's cheap cigars and of his standard breakfast: "I'm sick of your lightly buttered rye toast and eggs over lightly every goddamned morning. Would it kill you to have a waffle once in a while?" (626). Furthermore, Stu is angered that Mort controlled the trip too much—taking all the pictures, making all the plans, and forcing them to eat at nine Japanese restaurants.

The tensions between the two couples lead to verbal attacks and eventually to outright violence. Such a development is not uncommon in a play of this sort, for as Eric Bentley writes, farce is "notorious for its love of violent images."[15] In fact, Bentley cites the films of Charlie Chaplin (which Simon greatly admired in his youth) as an example of farce that employs violence for humorous purposes. As the most anarchic of dramatic forms, farce provides a vehicle, in Bentley's view, for a comic catharsis—a releasing of pent-up tensions and aggressions: "The violent release is comparable to the sudden relieving hiss of steam through a safety valve. Certainly, the mental energies involved are destructive, and in all comedy there remains something of destructive orgy, farce being the kind of comedy which disguises that fact least thoroughly."[16]

In "Visitors from Chicago," Simon invites his audience to share in such a comic catharsis, actually turning the Beverly Hills Hotel into a kind of war zone. His characters, who have become irrationally hostile toward one other, even adopt the vocabulary of combat. "That wasn't tennis out there," fumes Mort, after escorting his injured wife into the room. "That was war!" (616). When Gert asks for some Band-Aids and antiseptic after cutting her finger on a broken perfume bottle, Mort tells her to wait, saying, "Let's take one casualty at a time" (623). And after Gert bangs her head on the medicine cabinet and Mort cuts his foot on some broken glass, he exclaims, "Jesus, it's like Guadalcanal in here" (626). Losing their tempers, the two men also resort to physical attacks—kicking, biting, and punching each other. According to Bentley, one of the messages of farce is that man "may or may not be one of the more intelligent animals; he is certainly an animal, and not one of the least violent."[17] Simon's last playlet, with its outrageous verbal and physical attacks, confirms this fundamental message.

Like the other one-act comedies in *California Suite*, "Visitors from Chicago" concludes with a move toward reconciliation, but it is a bizarre kind of truce indeed. With a stranglehold on Stu, Mort announces that no one will leave the room until they have made peace with each other. "We came here friends and we're leaving friends. Now, tell me we're friends, you bastard!" (631). As the curtain falls, the other three characters exhort Stu to surrender and to promise that he will take another vacation with Mort and Beth the following year. The playlet thus concludes with a forced rapprochement, suggesting not so much a renewal of friendship as a temporary cessation of hostilities.

Whether his characters decide to make love (as do Diana and Sidney in "Visitors from London") or war (as do the Hollenders and the Franklyns in "Visitors from Chicago"), Simon stresses throughout *California Suite* the importance of reconciliation. In an imperfect world, he suggests, there will always be infidelities, divorces, arguments, and petty jealousies. But reconciliation—or at least a better understanding of one's fellow human beings—can make for greater peace of mind. This emphasis on reconciliation in four very different playlets may have prompted Simon to conclude, as he did in 1977, that *California Suite* was indeed his most sanguine comedy since *Barefoot in the Park*. "I'm trying to write about people who have not necessarily an optimistic view of life," he explained, "but certainly a hopeful one."[18]

CHAPTER EIGHT

Chapter Two

Although *Chapter Two* (1977) is a romantic comedy, it is also a cathartic play and one of Simon's most painfully autobiographical works.[1] In it the playwright deals with his enormous grief over the death of his wife, Joan, and with the problems surrounding his marriage several months later to his second wife, actress Marsha Mason. Simon's protagonist, a writer named George Schneider, is having difficulty reconciling his feelings of sorrow over the death of his wife, Barbara, with his new feelings of love for actress Jennie Malone. Rushing into marriage, George and Jennie are confronted with serious problems in their relationship, eventually learning that they must come to terms with the past if they are to begin "chapter two" in their lives. The play is notable not only for its examination of love and the process of bereavement but also for its self-reflexivity—that is, the writer's commentary on the craft of writing itself.

As a romantic comedy, *Chapter Two* is a curious hybrid. The play makes use of the standard Menandrian boy-meets-girl plot in act 1 and then shifts to Simon's favorite variation of the Menandrian framework—the "problem marriage" plot—in act 2. The first act concentrates on George Schneider's whirlwind—and often amusing—courtship of Jennie Malone, concluding with the couple's marriage. The second act, which is far more serious, examines the problems that the newlyweds are experiencing because of George's continued attachment to his first wife, and it closes, in traditional comedic fashion, with a renewal of the protagonist's marriage to Jennie.

In portraying his romantic pair, Simon adopts a different approach to staging, presenting the protagonists' apartments (which are located on opposite sides of Manhattan) on stage simultaneously. The set design enables the audience to contrast George's apartment—and hence his character—with Jennie's. Despite its comfortable decor, George's apartment is cold and inhospitable: the heat has not been turned on, the refrigerator contains spoiled food, and pictures of his deceased wife are prominently displayed. George's home is a visible sign of his bereavement. Jennie's apartment, on the other hand, is warm and inviting, reflecting her more hopeful spirits. Even when Jennie leaves town to get a divorce from her first husband, she arranges for the doorman to turn on her heat, for her plants to be watered, and for her refrigerator to be stocked with food. Although the protagonists have both recently undergone a traumatic experience, Jennie is clearly ready to pick up the pieces and move on with her life, whereas George is not. As critic Clive Barnes observed, the play is about "a woman who wants to seize happiness and a man resolutely 'trying to hold on to self-pity.'"[2]

Like most romantic comedies, *Chapter Two* emphasizes the obstacles that the lovers must overcome before they can be happily united. Chief among these obstacles is the emotional insecurity of both characters. Still mourning the loss of his wife, George has deep misgivings about beginning a new relationship, believing that he hasn't yet put the pieces of his life back together. Jennie Malone is also pictured as emotionally vulnerable, having just undergone a painful divorce from her husband, Gus. As she says to George's brother in act 2, "Who picked me out as the stable one, Leo? I've just come from five years of analysis and a busted marriage."[3]

Another obstacle for George and Jennie is their concern about the whirlwind nature of their courtship. The characters do not really know each other well, having been acquainted for only two weeks before deciding to get married. Extremely nervous on the morning of the ceremony, George cuts himself shaving and then asks, "Who is she, Leo? I'm marrying a girl, I don't know who she is" (702). Jennie's friend Faye Medwick likewise questions Jennie about her impulsive decision to marry George, asking, "Why are you getting married to a man you've known two and a half weeks who was married to a woman he idolized for twelve years?" (694). This rapid courtship reflects Simon's own experience with actress Marsha Mason, whom he met during the rehearsals for his play *The Good Doctor* (1973). According to Simon, after he and Marsha began dating each other, they were married within three weeks. "If I had thought about it a lot, I probably wouldn't have done it, but I plunged into marriage because my instincts told me it was right, that Marsha was the right girl."[4]

Although the swiftness of the courtship presents difficulties for Jennie and George, the major problem that confronts them is George's deep-seated guilt about their relationship. He simply cannot accept feeling happy again so quickly after Barbara's death. George's love for Jennie, no matter how strong, seems to be a betrayal of his first wife and a sign that he wants to forget her. He tells Jennie that he resents her for expecting happiness and for making him feel so guilty: "And most of all, I resent not being able to say in front of you . . . that I miss Barbara so much" (714). Because George's guilt is such a formidable obstacle, the "boy wins girl" portion of Simon's plot occurs not with the couple's wedding in act

1 (as it would in a traditional romantic comedy) but with the renewal of George and Jennie's marriage in act 2, after a troubled honeymoon, a major argument, and a brief separation from each other.

In romantic comedies, as Paul H. Grawe has noted, love and romance sometimes serve as devices of education.[5] The characters learn something about themselves and the world around them, particularly about the meaning of love itself. In *Chapter Two* Jennie learns that she cannot replace George's first wife, Barbara; nor can she force George to "opt for happiness," (727), as she calls it. She can only assure him of her devotion and of her determination to make their marriage work. By the end of the play, George likewise becomes more educated about the nature of love. He learns that love is a healing force—even a source of salvation—and that he is foolish to pull away from Jennie, when she is exactly the person that he needs in his life. Asking himself what would happen if he returned to Jennie and started their marriage all over again, he finds that the answer is very simple: "I would be happy!" (736).

Like many romantic comedies, *Chapter Two* includes a second pair of would-be lovers (George's brother, Leo Schneider, and Jennie's friend, Faye Medwick), but some critics have found fault with Simon's use of a subplot involving an attempted extramarital affair between these two secondary characters. Richard Eder argues that the farcical seduction scenes between Leo and Faye "virtually wreck the second-act scenes between George and Jennie. They have no relation to them."[6] Robert K. Johnson, however, defends Simon's use of the subplot, asserting that it does bear a relation to the main story. Specifically, Johnson points to Faye's new awareness that marital problems must be confronted openly and that she must begin to communicate with her husband (a lesson that George and Jennie learn after their honeymoon).[7] Leo, on the other hand, fails to learn anything new about human relationships, resorting to promiscuous sexual activity instead of addressing his personal problems directly. Leo thus finally serves in the play not only as a confidant to his brother, George, but as a major foil to the protagonist.

Despite being a romantic comedy, *Chapter Two* offers a realistic portrait of the process of bereavement. As in *The Gingerbread Lady,* Simon puts into practice his belief that tragic and comic elements can be combined effectively in the same play. Struggling to deal with the death of his wife, George Schneider exhibits common symptoms of bereavement—preoccupation with the deceased, sadness, disbelief, and anger. Rather than finding an escape through his travels in Europe, he deliberately went back to the sites that he and Barbara once visited together, even telling Leo that he found himself wandering the streets of London looking for her. Unable to accept his wife's death, George also admits to feelings of anger. "In Rome I got sore at her—I mean *really* mad. How dare she do a thing like this to me? I would *never* do a thing like that to her. Never! Like a nut, walking up the Via Veneto one night, cursing my dead wife" (639).

But the primary symptom of bereavement which George reveals in the play is that of guilt—guilt for being alive and for trying to reach out for happiness again, when his loved one is dead. In a 1991 interview Simon emphasized the terrible guilt that he himself felt after beginning a new relationship with Marsha Mason within months of Joan Simon's death. Although his daughters encouraged him to move on with his life, "still you get that kick of guilt . . . much like the survivors of the Holocaust when those who lived felt guilty all their lives." According to Simon, George Schneider, in *Chapter Two,* was likewise unable "to give himself the enjoyment and the latitude of exploring this new relationship without always pulling in the guilt of being alive and his wife being dead." Writing the play was finally a cathartic experience, said the playwright, because it helped him to rid himself of his own guilt "by sharing it with the world."[8]

Simon's comment about guilt and the survivors of the Holocaust also serves as a reminder of the Jewish subtext in *Chapter Two.* Whereas Jennie points to her Catholic upbringing as the reason for her organization and self-discipline, George and Leo subtly reveal their Jewish background. George plans to marry Jennie in the chambers of Judge Ira Markovitz—the kind of neutral setting, argues Daniel Walden, "usually chosen by secular and Reformed Jews for marriages."[9] When Leo admits to an oversolicitous interest in his brother's welfare, he says, "I don't know what the hell I'm doing in publicity. I was born to be a Jewish mother" (687). Walden also suggests that after Barbara's death, George has been "wearing his heart on his sleeve, indulging in suffering, in the way many Russian Jews did in the *shtetlach* [the Jewish ghettoes of Eastern Europe]."[10] Jennie herself is well aware of George's guilt complex and his apparent need to suffer. Near the end of the play, when George packs his bags to leave for Los Angeles, she remarks angrily, "I don't know what you expect to find out there, except a larger audience for your two shows a day of suffering" (727). In Walden's view, George Schneider is thus pictured not simply as a bereaved widower but as a kind of Everyman and an embodiment of the suffering Jew.

CHAPTER TWO

The reconciliation between George and Jennie in the play's final scene provides the traditional happy ending that one expects from a romantic comedy, but it also signals the close of George's period of mourning—an experience that Simon has depicted with considerable realism. J. William Worden, in *Grief Counseling and Grief Therapy,* identifies four primary tasks of bereavement: (1) "to accept the reality of the loss," (2) "to work through to the pain of grief," (3) "to adjust to an environment in which the deceased is missing," and (4) "to emotionally relocate the deceased and move on with life."[11] In *Chapter Two* George has successfully worked his way through the grieving process, accomplishing these four tasks of bereavement. He has anguished over his wife's death and has gradually accepted it. He has slowly adjusted to a world without Barbara at his side. Most importantly, he has channeled his emotional energies into a new relationship with Jennie Malone—the last and most difficult task of bereavement.

Freud once wrote that "grief should free the bereaved from the dead,"[12] and this is ultimately what happens to George Schneider in Simon's play. The final conversation between George and Jennie, mixed as it is with humor and avowals of affection, emphasizes not only the reconciliation of the two lovers but also the healing that eventually comes through the process of bereavement itself. By the end of the play George is ready to come to terms with his past, to conclude his period of mourning, and to reach out for the happiness that lies directly in front of him. The protagonist's successful movement through the grieving process is accentuated in *Chapter Two* by the change in seasons (the play begins in winter and closes in midspring) and also by the title of his new novel, *Falling Into Place,* which George starts to read aloud to Jennie at the final curtain.

Before he met Jennie Malone, George was convinced that his world had fallen apart completely. But now he is struck by a sense of harmony and of things coming together at last.

Besides serving as a cathartic drama, *Chapter Two* is one of the first of Simon's plays to deal with an important self-reflexive topic: the writer's account of the craft of writing itself. Although several of Simon's earlier characters are identified as writers (e.g., Oscar Madison, in *The Odd Couple,* is a sportswriter; Bill Warren, in *California Suite,* is a screenwriter), their occupations do not play an integral role in the comedies. Simon's experimental drama *The Good Doctor* (1973), an adaptation of short stories by Anton Chekhov, was his first attempt to deal more seriously with the subject of the writer's art. In this play the figure of "the Writer" (who introduces the sketches and takes various parts within them) expounds on the writing process in several key monologues, defining himself not so much as Chekhov but as the universal writer. He reveals his problem with writer's block, his alienation, and his relentless compulsion to write: "What force is it that compels me to write so incessantly, day after day, page after page, story after story? And the answer is quite simple: I have no choice. I am a writer."[13]

Although *Chapter Two* does not contain explicit monologues on writing, the play comments indirectly on writers and the nature of their craft. Like Simon himself, George Schneider is a popular author who makes a comfortable living but who yearns to write serious literature that will be appreciated by posterity. Using the pen name Kenneth Blakely-Hill, George writes spy novels that can be found in many drugstores and airports but not in libraries. Under his own name he has written two serious novels that were commercial failures, but it is these books in which he takes the most pride.

CHAPTER TWO

Recognizing George's desire to be regarded as a serious, and enduring, writer, Jennie gives him a special present before their wedding—copies of his two books bound elegantly in leather. "Guaranteed to last as long as Dickens and Twain" (690), she says. George is genuinely moved by this gift, since his deepest aspiration is to be not a commercial success but a writer whose work will be read and remembered for many years to come.

The protagonist's occupation as writer directly affects the way that he communicates with and behaves toward others. During their first phone conversations Jennie is aware that George has a gift for words. "You're a writer, that's for sure," she tells him. "I took English Lit. This is what they call 'repartee,' isn't it?" (660). George's identity as writer also causes him to ask personal questions, to "pry incessantly"—something that he terms an "occupational hazard" (660). In addition, it creates in him a desire for perfection, a need to revise both his fiction and his personal life. According to Jennie, he even revised his latest book during their honeymoon in Barbados. Because he is a writer, George essentially sees his own life as a book—a manuscript that is partly written but over which, quite frighteningly, he at times has no control. "Okay, Leo, my sweet baby brother, I'm back," he says at the start of the play. "Chapter Two in the life of George Schneider. Where the hell do I begin?" (639).

Viewed within the larger context of Simon's work, *Chapter Two* is an intriguingly autobiographical play, not only because it deals with the playwright's complicated feelings about loss, bereavement, and renewal, but also because it begins to reveal who Simon is as a writer—his talents, his habits, his dreams—especially his desire to be taken seriously by the literary world and to be remembered kindly by posterity. In later years Simon would explore this self-reflexive topic of the writer in more detail, most notably in the 1980s in the Brighton Beach trilogy, in which the character of Eugene Morris Jerome serves as the playwright's alter ego, and also in two more recent dramas: *Jake's Women* (1992), an expressionistic portrait of a writer's inner self, and *Laughter on the 23rd Floor* (1993), an account of a group of television comedy writers, based on Simon's own experience working for Sid Caesar's *Your Show of Shows*.

CHAPTER NINE

The Brighton Beach Trilogy

Brighton Beach Memoirs (1983), *Biloxi Blues* (1985), and *Broadway Bound* (1986) are a series of semi-autobiographical plays that chronicle the life of Eugene Morris Jerome (Simon's alter ego) from his adolescence in Brooklyn during the Depression to his basic training experience in World War II to his eventual entry into show business. The first of Simon's comedies to present characters who are explicitly Jewish, these plays explore subjects such as sibling rivalry, marital conflict, ethnicity, and anti-Semitism. But Simon's principal themes throughout the trilogy are (1) the coming of age of Eugene Jerome, including the young man's development as a writer, and (2) the importance of family unity. In *Brighton Beach Memoirs,* which is an idealized account of his boyhood, Simon emphasizes that during troubled times one can find security through the strength of the family. In *Biloxi Blues* he delineates Eugene Jerome's growth as a human being and a writer after the protagonist leaves home to serve in the army. Finally, in *Broadway Bound,* the most poignant of the three plays, Simon focuses on the breakup of the Jerome family unit and on the cautious optimism that the protagonist feels as he moves into manhood.

Brighton Beach Memoirs

Critic T. E. Kalem has referred to *Brighton Beach Memoirs* as "Neil Simon's love letter to his past."[1] Indeed, the play is a nostalgic (and rose-colored) look at the playwright's experience growing up in a

Jewish family in New York City during the Depression. The title itself has a double meaning: it refers to the journal, or "secret memoirs,"[2] that the adolescent Eugene Jerome is keeping in order to prepare himself to become a writer; it also refers to the play as a whole—to Simon's own recollection of his childhood experiences in New York. In this second respect, *Brighton Beach Memoirs* is a memory play in the tradition of Tennessee Williams's *The Glass Menagerie.* Set in 1937, the drama offers, to be sure, a somewhat idealized view of the Jerome family, yet Simon identifies this idealized vision as the play's primary source of appeal. As he told an interviewer in 1991, *Brighton Beach Memoirs,* aside from *The Odd Couple,* is performed more than any play that he has ever written. "There is something about the idealization of the family in that play that we all dream about. . . . It's like looking back on your family album and seeing it better than it was."[3]

Departing in *Brighton Beach Memoirs* from the conventions of the realistic theater, Simon employs a narrator who speaks directly to the audience. In a series of monologues and asides, Eugene Jerome breaks through the imaginary "fourth wall" onstage, deliberately calling attention to the fact that the audience is witnessing a play and not reality. Like Tom Wingfield in *The Glass Menagerie,* Eugene introduces the play's characters to the audience and offers a running commentary on them. When Stanley Jerome first makes an appearance, Eugene says, "My brother Stan. He's okay. You'll like him" (500). And when Jack Jerome arrives, he announces, "I would now like to introduce my father, a real hard worker. He was born at the age of forty-two" (507). According to John Beaufort, who reviewed the original production of the play, Eugene is "a one-man Greek chorus in brown knickers and scuffed sneakers. As both guide and protagonist, he furnishes the ideal liaison between the 1983 audience and the 1937 world of Brighton Beach."[4]

In his role as narrator, Eugene also helps to preserve the play's comic perspective, forming a bond with everyone in the theater. (As Simon himself has noted, the protagonist is actually the only humorous character in the play.)[5] Eugene speaks to the audience "confidentially" at the opening of the drama, saying, "Listen, I hope you don't repeat this to anybody . . . What I'm telling you are my secret memoirs" (487). Then he proceeds to divulge some of his deepest secrets, such as the fact that he is having lustful thoughts about his pretty cousin Nora. By turning the audience into his confidants, Eugene immediately creates sympathy for himself—especially when his mother nags him or when she plays favorites with his sickly cousin, Laurie. Escaping to his room after a scolding from his mother and a threatened blow to the head, Eugene tells the audience, "You see why I want to write all this down? In case I grow up all twisted and warped, the world will know why" (488).

Eugene's mother, Kate Jerome, is in some ways a stereotypical Jewish mother. She is strong and assertive, she is a meticulous housekeeper, and she is immensely concerned about caring for her family. But Kate has certain unflattering qualities as well. As Ellen Schiff notes, Kate "wields guilt like a scalpel" in order to manipulate others.[6] She is prejudiced toward members of other ethnic groups, especially the Irish people who live across the street, whom she describes as a "filthy bunch" (488). Even more disturbing is Kate's cool treatment of Eugene. She sends him on errands and constantly gives him orders, but she doesn't display any outward affection for him. According to Simon, his own mother, Mamie Simon, had difficulty showing her love for her children: "I don't remember ever being hugged by my mother as far back as being a child," he recalled. "I always knew that she loved me, but she was unable to show emotion."[7]

Simon's portrait of his father, Irving Simon, is more idealized, for Jack Jerome is not the stereotypical Jewish father who meekly follows in the footsteps of his dominant wife. Instead, he is a strong and dependable head of the household.[8] Working long hours to support his extended family, Jack is still willing to listen to others when they have problems (e.g., when Nora argues with Blanche about wanting to quit school or when Stanley is fired from his job). It is obvious that everyone in the family looks up to Jack, viewing him as compassionate, fair, and supportive. Even when he loses one of his two jobs and worries that he won't be able to feed his large family, Jack doesn't despair. "What God gives us to deal with, we deal with" (523), he declares. Jack is also capable of seeing the larger picture. No matter how great his own troubles are during the Depression, he realizes that life is much worse for millions of Jews in Europe, some of whom are his own relatives. Noting that Hitler has already invaded Austria, Jack fears that the entire world will soon be at war. "We're already in it," he tells his family. "Not us maybe. But friends, relatives. If you're Jewish, you've got a cousin suffering *somewhere* in the world" (523).

The emphasis in *Brighton Beach Memoirs* is on comic survival. Eugene's family is beset, to be sure, by some serious problems. Jack suffers a mild heart attack in act 2, making it impossible for him to work; Stan loses his salary while gambling and leaves the house in shame; Blanche and Nora are still estranged from one another after their argument about Nora's schooling; and Kate and her sister Blanche clash over Blanche's dependence on them, with Kate even blaming her sister for Jack's illness. Yet these problems are largely resolved by the end of the play. Not only does Jack appear to be getting stronger, but also a series of reconciliations takes place that brings the family together again. Kate Jerome, in particular, voices her belief in the importance of family unity, especially during times of hardship. "This is a family," she asserts. "The world doesn't survive without families" (526).

Some critics, like Frank Rich, have accused Simon of "Pollyannaism," arguing that the play's happy ending is too pat and that the Jerome family's problems are solved too easily.[9] It should be remembered, however, that in *Brighton Beach Memoirs* Simon has chosen to emphasize not a realistic account of past events but Eugene's memories of those events—memories that are largely informed by the protagonist's youthful and comic spirit. Given Eugene's tendency to find humor in almost every subject, it is only natural that the family's numerous problems at the end of the play (including the announcement that seven of Jack's relatives have escaped from Poland and will need to stay with them) would be perceived as amusing and as capable of being resolved. Furthermore, as Ellen Schiff has noted, the upbeat conclusion of *Brighton Beach Memoirs* is actually reminiscent of a number of American Jewish family plays, from Sylvia Regan's *Morning Star* (1940) to Israel Horovitz's *A Rosen By Any Other Name* (1987).[10]

The play's other main theme—the coming of age of Eugene Jerome—is illustrated in part through the protagonist's growing awareness of his sexuality. Some of the comedy's humor derives from Eugene's erotic thoughts about his cousin Nora and his preoccupation with sex in general. During the dinner scene in act 1, when Eugene keeps dropping his napkin so that he can look at Nora's legs under the table, he claims that he can see "halfway up her thighs that led to the Golden Palace of the Himalayas" (516). By the end of the play Eugene's crush on Nora is over, but his interest in sex is undiminished. When Stanley presents him with a special gift—a picture of a naked woman—Eugene exuberantly declares that he has seen "the Golden Palace of the Himalayas" and that "puberty is over" (593).

Eugene's coming of age is also revealed in his budding sense of himself as a writer. "One day I'm going to put all this in a book or a play," he claims. "I'm going to be a writer like Ring Lardner or somebody—that's if things don't work out first with the Yankees, or the Cubs, or the Red Sox, or maybe possibly the Tigers . . . If I get down to the St. Louis Browns, then I'll definitely be a writer" (486–87). Although Eugene's vision of his future is tentative and immature, he is beginning to think and behave like a writer. Observant of others, he makes notes in his journal of what various family members do or say. He also uses writing as a means of self-expression, carefully recording his private thoughts in his "secret memoirs." Eugene even has a sense of a future audience for his work: "I, Eugene M. Jerome, have committed a mortal sin by lusting after my cousin Nora. I can tell you all this now because I'll be dead when you're reading it" (496). The actual audience in the theater is witnessing a play, of course, but at the same time it is essentially "reading" Eugene's memoirs, sharing his innermost thoughts and feelings. The members of the audience are not merely observers, therefore, but the protagonist's allies, his confidants, and the ultimate "readers" upon whom a writer must depend.

Biloxi Blues

Moving away from the domestic drama of *Brighton Beach Memoirs,* Simon focuses his next play, *Biloxi Blues* (1985), on Eugene

Jerome's basic training experience in the army during World War II. Like the first play, *Biloxi Blues* is dominated by the theme of Eugene Jerome's coming of age. Indeed, the opening scene on the troop train effectively introduces the motif of the journey, or the movement from innocence to experience. Eugene, now six years older in 1943, still reveals his innocence in an engaging manner, letting the audience know that he has never even been away from home before. "In my duffel bag are twelve pot roast sandwiches my mother gave me,"[11] he admits. He also claims that he has three primary goals while in the army: to become a writer, to avoid being killed, and to lose his virginity. During the course of the play Eugene is initiated into army life but also into an adult world filled with sex, love, cruelty, and prejudice. And it is here, in this adult world far from Brighton Beach, that Eugene truly begins to find his identity as a writer.

As John Beaufort noted in his review of the play, *Biloxi Blues* is "a traditional barracks-room comedy, replete with GI humor and one of those sergeants who insults, humiliates, and bullies his awkward squads into obedience."[12] Like Ira Levin's *No Time for Sergeants* (1955), the play depicts the initiation of an innocent young man into the rigors of military life. Eugene must contend with the crudity of the other soldiers, the miserable food in the mess hall, and army discipline, especially as it is imposed by his fanatical drill sergeant, Merwin J. Toomey. Pictured as every soldier's nightmare, Sergeant Toomey forces the soldiers to do one hundred push-ups for the smallest infraction, makes them go on a fifteen-mile hike through reptile-infested swamps on the night of their arrival, and insists that they eat every bite of disgusting army food that is on their plate. "I was weaned on Discipline," brags Toomey. "I sucked Discipline from my mother's breast" (678).

The major foil to Sergeant Toomey in the play is Eugene's Jewish friend Arnold Epstein, a sensitive, intellectual young man who constantly challenges Toomey's authority and, as a result, spends much of his time during basic training cleaning latrines. In contrast to the drill sergeant, Epstein supports individualism, freedom of thought, and humane treatment of one's fellow man—all of which are glaringly absent from the barracks-room environment. Epstein is especially appalled by the "Neanderthal" tactics that Toomey employs to impose discipline on the men, telling the sergeant that he doesn't believe it is necessary to humiliate the soldiers in order to motivate them to perform. Eugene actually learns important lessons from both of these men. From Sergeant Toomey he learns the necessity of discipline in the military. As Eugene wryly observes, "If nobody obeys orders, I'll bet we wouldn't have more than twelve or thirteen soldiers fighting the war . . . We'd have headlines like 'Corporal Stanley Leiberman invades Sicily'" (623). From Arnold Epstein, Eugene learns the importance of preserving one's dignity, one's sense of compassion, and one's individuality—even when the military machine threatens to turn its men into robots.

One of the most disturbing aspects of army life that Eugene encounters in Biloxi, Mississippi, is the prejudice that infects the troops. For the first time in his life the protagonist is exposed to the cruelty of anti-Semitism. Pvt. Joseph Wykowski, for instance, repeatedly makes bigoted remarks like "Jewish guys are all homos" and "It's always the Jews who end up with the money" (634). Although Eugene—perhaps because of his engaging personality—is able to avoid serious conflict, his friend Arnold Epstein is the victim of both verbal and physical attacks. Disgusted by such behavior, Eugene does not take any action against the offenders, preferring to remain "sort of neutral . . . like Switzerland" (636). Afterwards, however, the protagonist hates himself even more than he does the anti-Semitic soldiers, for he realizes that it was his moral responsibility to stand up for Epstein—a friend and "a fellow Jew" (636).

Eugene also witnesses homophobia in the army and must come to terms with his own feelings about homosexuals. When one of the soldiers, James Hennesey, is given a dishonorable discharge and three months in prison for committing a homosexual act, some of the men are openly prejudiced. Wykowski maintains that no one in America will give a gay man like Hennesey a job, and Selridge argues that the army is crazy to discharge homosexuals: "They should keep them together in one outfit. 'The Fruit Brigade' . . . Make them nurses or something" (689–90). Though dismayed by such bigotry, Eugene realizes that he must also learn to deal with his own intolerance. In his memoirs Eugene even writes that he suspects that Epstein might be homosexual, "and it bothers me that it bothers me" (665).

Besides being exposed to prejudice in the military, Eugene is initiated into the mysteries of sex and love. During the play's second act Simon describes the protagonist's encounters with a pair of female characters who are presented as opposites: Rowena, the prostitute who provides Eugene with his first sexual experience, and Daisy Hannigan, the innocent Catholic girl with whom he falls briefly in love. Though relieved to have lost his virginity (one of his three basic goals in joining the army), Eugene learns from Rowena that he never wants to pay for the experience again, concluding that "[i]t just cheapens the whole idea of sex" (671). Instead, he finds much more fulfillment in his platonic relationship with Daisy Hannigan, who, in his mind, has a lovelier name than Fitzgerald's Daisy Buchanan. Although Eugene, like Gatsby, ultimately loses his Daisy, never seeing her again after he is shipped out to Europe, it is clear that this brief relationship with the girl is an important rite of passage for the protagonist.

In describing Eugene's coming of age, Simon also concentrates on the young man's development as a writer. Unlike the rather cocky youth in *Brighton Beach Memoirs,* Eugene Jerome discovers that he has a great deal to learn about being a writer. According to William A. Henry III, "the Eugene of *Biloxi Blues* knows how little he knows. He is aware enough of the larger world to realize how many perils, including war, may bar his path to glory."[13] Edwin Wilson adds that "Eugene is beginning to discover the price one pays for being a writer."[14] For one thing, the protagonist is learning about the dangers of being a mere observer of life rather than a participant. Arnold Epstein rebukes him for not getting involved, for standing around watching others and then "scribbling" in his journal rather than taking sides. Eugene agrees with Epstein, admitting that sometimes he feels invisible. "Like The Shadow. I can see everyone else but they can't see me. That's what I think writers are. Sort of invisible" (644).

Eugene also learns that as a writer he must inevitably use other people, violating their privacy at times and turning them into raw material for his art. After the fantasy game (in which the soldiers reveal how they would want to spend their last few days on earth), Eugene confesses that he is somewhat ashamed to have recorded the men's secret desires in his journal. He feels especially guilty for the words he has written about Arnold Epstein's sexual orientation, for when the other soldiers find Eugene's journal and read it aloud, they automatically jump to the conclusion that Epstein is homosexual. Eugene suddenly realizes that a writer needs to exercise caution, because people usually believe what they read. Yet when he tears the offending page out of his memoirs, Epstein chides him, saying, "That's a mistake, Gene . . . Once you start compromising your thoughts, you're a candidate for mediocrity" (670).

Having no desire to offend his reading audience, Eugene wishes to be a responsible writer. But he must somehow learn to balance his concern about the effect of his words with a determination to express himself truthfully. As Frank Rich suggested in his review of the play, this tension between the desire to please an audience and the desire for honest self-expression is one that Simon himself was well aware of, particularly given his status as a commercially successful dramatist. Viewing Eugene's growth as a writer as parallel to that of the playwright himself, Rich hoped that in the future Simon would continue to heed Arnold Epstein's advice and refuse to be "a candidate for mediocrity."[15]

At the end of *Biloxi Blues* Eugene is once again traveling on a troop train—a framing device which emphasizes the broader journey that he is actually taking. Although the protagonist still has much to learn, he is clearly approaching manhood and is well on his way to becoming a serious writer. Having sustained a back injury in a jeep accident in England, Eugene never sees any combat during World War II. Instead, the army gives him a job writing for the GI newspaper *Stars and Stripes,* making the protagonist a professional writer for the first time in his life. According to critic Alan Cooper, Simon himself began to hone his writing skills during his service in the Army Air Force by covering sporting events for the military. In Cooper's estimation, "the army had defined [Simon] as a writer."[16] Surely in *Biloxi Blues* the same can finally be said for Simon's alter ego, Eugene Morris Jerome. Not only has the army begun to initiate Eugene into adulthood, but it also has explicitly defined him as a writer.

Broadway Bound

Comparing Simon with Eugene O'Neill (Simon's narrator and alter ego is named Eugene), scholars such as Jackson R. Bryer have suggested that *Brighton Beach Memoirs* is Simon's *Ah, Wilderness!,* while *Broadway Bound* is his *Long Day's Journey Into Night.* In the former play Simon treats his family in a comic and idealized manner, whereas in the latter he confronts his family more seriously and realistically.[17] Simon has even admitted that he could not have written *Broadway Bound* while his parents were still alive. Calling it "a play of forgiveness" and "an attempt . . . to understand my family and my own origins,"[18] the author also agreed that this final play in the Brighton Beach trilogy was essentially a love letter to his mother.

On one level, *Broadway Bound* is the lighthearted story of how Eugene Jerome and his brother, Stan, make their entry into show business in the late 1940s, working as a team of comedy writers for radio. Simon thus continues to explore the dominant theme of his trilogy—the coming of age of Eugene Jerome. On another level, though, the play is about the painful dissolution of Kate and Jack Jerome's thirty-three-year marriage and the breakup of the Jerome family unit. According to Allan Wallach, who reviewed the original production of the drama, "it is as though a familiar Simon comedy were intertwined with an Arthur Miller play."[19]

The play's title, *Broadway Bound,* suggests optimism and the American success myth, yet certain members of the Jerome family

ack. Although Ben's wife is sick and doctors have advised
ve to Florida, the old man has no desire to join her—
since, thanks to Blanche, his wife will be violating his
rinciples by living in relative luxury. Eugene's youthful
attachment to Josie, on the other hand, is sharply con-
h the troubled union of Kate and Jack. Having fallen seri-
ove, Eugene is beginning to think about marriage for the
but he yearns for the intimacy that has somehow eluded
arents and grandparents. Without intimacy, he tells the
life is "just breakfast, lunch, dinner, and a good night's
st people would settle for that. Most people do . . . I was
d not to be most people" (790).

picting the marital strife between Kate and Jack Jerome,
ecially focuses on Kate Jerome's disappointment, pain,
courage, and in this sense, the play truly is a tribute, or
, to Simon's mother. As numerous critics have observed,
Bound contains a key scene toward which the rest of the
ds—one that creates a loving connection between mother
his memorable scene takes place in act 2, as Kate recalls
many years ago when she went to the Primrose Ballroom
d with movie star George Raft. (The incident is taken from
Simon's mother, Mamie Simon, who actually danced not
ge Raft but with the comedian George Burns, himself a
lroom dancer.) 25 After Kate relates this Cinderella story
ant monologue, Eugene invites his mother to dance with
urmurs, "You're so graceful, Mom . . . I never knew you
raceful" (788). As a writer, Eugene cannot help seeing
's story as perfect material for a movie. But this time he
move beyond the role of witty observer and participate

question this myth. Eugene's grandfather, Ben, an avid reader of
Trotsky, is quick to denounce all capitalistic enterprises. He is especially critical of his daughter Blanche, who has remarried and now
wears a mink coat and rides in a chauffeured Cadillac. "I can't enjoy
the benefits of a society that made my daughter rich and starves half
the people in the country,"[20] Ben declares. Jack Jerome, Eugene's
father, also questions the dream of success implicit in the play's title
but from a different vantage point. He believes that his sons' dream
of breaking into show business is "a one in a million shot" (741) and
that there is no financial security in it. "You don't keep a roof over
your head doing what you *want* to do" (741), Jack insists.

As Eugene pursues his dream, he begins to think more seriously about the nature and purpose of comedy, learning from those
around him. His mother, Kate Jerome, equates comedy with laughter, apparently believing that comedy can have a healing effect.
Eugene's socialist grandfather, Ben, claims that comedy should
make people "aware" and that the best form of comedy is political
satire. The protagonist's brother, Stan, tends to define comedy in
terms of its structure, arguing that the two essential ingredients of
any comedy are conflict and desire and that comedy must be believe-
able in order to be funny. Eugene himself is convinced that comedy
is a simply a reflection of real life, telling the audience, "There's so
much material in this house. Maybe I don't have to become a writer.
If only I could get enough people to pay for seats in the living room"
(729).

Yet Eugene also learns, as he did in *Biloxi Blues,* that it is risky
to use the people to whom he is closest as material (and audience) for
his comedic art. When the brothers' first comedy sketch is broadcast
on the radio, Kate fails to laugh at the funny lines, and Ben denigrates

such a show for offering lighthearted entertainment when "three quarters of the world [is] in economic slavery" (758). The worst review comes from Jack Jerome, who is outraged that his sons have used members of their own family as models for the comedy sketch. They have depicted a grandfather who falls asleep anywhere (just like Ben), a mother whose speech patterns are exactly like Kate's, and a father whose business is "in ladies' pajamas" (770). Particularly offended by the risqué reference to ladies' pajamas, since it recalls his own infidelity, Jack declares that he will never forgive his sons for exposing him to public ridicule.

Many of Simon's comedies, as we have seen, adopt the Menandrian "problem marriage" plot, often concluding with the renewal of the protagonists' marriage. In the autobiographical *Broadway Bound,* however, Simon directly confronts the stormy marriage of his own parents, Irving and Mamie Simon, making no attempt to supply his drama with a traditional comedic ending. During the author's childhood, as Simon explains in *Rewrites,* his father left home and separated from his mother on at least eight occasions, remaining absent from a month to a year each time.[21] Although Irving Simon was not physically abusive, he frequently treated his wife in a way "that would embarrass her, frighten her, or humiliate her. He could sleep next to her for a month without uttering a single word to her."[22] Eventually Irving Simon left the household for good and began living with another woman. Simon writes: "I view the marriage between Mamie and Irving Simon through a child's memory, a recollection distorted by the pain and ugliness and fury of their clashes and the sudden idyllic joy and happiness I often saw them share together. The truth, I'm certain, lies somewhere between the two images."[23] It is this truth that Simon attempts to reveal in *Broadway Bound.*

In *Brighton Beach Memoirs* Jack Jerom man who held his family together during *Broadway Bound* he is portrayed as the mar the dissolution of the Jerome family. After years as a cutter in the garment district, J midlife crisis. Restless and discontented, he a in an extra-marital affair, explaining to Kat gave him an escape from his narrow life. A feels the need to make a new beginning for children to raise," he tells Ben near the end ing waiting out there for me except one th (792).

Kate recognizes her own inability to midlife crisis or to compete with a rival s tress—a woman who is well educated an displays an interest in the world beyond h ditional Jewish mother, Kate has taken c thirty years and raised their two children right books or traveled any further in t could take her" (747). Set in the post-V thus provides a portrait, as Frank Rich s "single-minded purpose and the Old Wo maternal mission are fast becoming obs

The stormy relationship between K taposed with two other relationships in marriage to Kate's mother—a woman w and (2) Eugene's romantic attachment t character who, like Kate's mother, ne estrangement from his wife mirrors the

tenderly in his mother's story, helping her to relive that fairy tale evening by dancing with Kate himself.

Critic Frank Rich called this scene "the indisputable peak" of *Broadway Bound,*[26] while Douglas Watt termed it "the most brilliant and affecting set piece in the entire Simon canon."[27] Although Jack Jerome is about to desert Kate (and indeed he leaves in the very next scene), she comes alive in this dance sequence, recapturing her youth and revealing herself as the graceful, desirable young woman she once was. According to Jack Kroll, the dance scene "evokes a time of romantic possibility that contrasts with [Kate's] current life. . . . We feel the waste of a woman's unlived life and the shock of a young man who feels in his arms the repressed rhythm of that life."[28] Particularly heart-rending to Eugene, of course, is the realization that in dancing with his mother, he is serving as a stand-in for his father.

Ironically, the development of Eugene as a writer—particularly his early success writing comedy with his brother, Stan—contributes further to the breakup of the Jerome family unit. In act 1, two humorous scenes in which Eugene and Stan try to come up with an idea for their first professional comedy sketch are strategically placed on either side of the major argument between Kate and Jack. By arranging the scenes in this manner, Simon calls attention to the two levels of his drama, emphasizing how humor and anguish can exist side by side, even within a single dwelling. But he also connects the two levels of his story thematically, tying them to the final breakup of the Jerome household. By the end of the play Eugene and Stan have not only written a number of comedy sketches for radio, but they have also landed a job on *The Phil Silvers Show.* Yet their success causes them to move permanently out of their home in

Brighton Beach in order to pursue their careers in New York. While Jack leaves the house out of frustration and unhappiness, Eugene and Stan depart with excitement and optimism. The result, however, is ultimately the same: the Jeromes will never again live together as a family.

Unlike *Brighton Beach Memoirs, Broadway Bound* thus closes in a realistic rather than comedic fashion. There is no happy ending, no neat resolution to the family's difficulties. In the final scene Eugene takes his suitcase and exits from the house as Kate waxes her grandmother's table—a beloved heirloom that, ironically for Kate, represents family history and unity. Jack has abandoned her, Ben has moved to Florida, and now her two sons are leaving the house for good. But having made his passage into manhood, Eugene is finally able to put his mother's experience in perspective, recognizing that there were also moments of happiness in Kate's life. On the whole, says Eugene, "she considers herself a pretty lucky woman. After all, she did once dance with George Raft" (803).

In a review of *Brighton Beach Memoirs,* Walter Kerr wrote that Simon "lets us watch the comic mind growing up"—that he, in effect, offers his own portrait of the artist as a young man.[29] This is true not only of *Brighton Beach Memoirs* but of the entire Brighton Beach trilogy. In the first play Eugene is introduced as an amusing, rather cocky boy, quick to find humor in the multiple problems that beset his Jewish family. In *Biloxi Blues,* he is pictured as a funny but sensitive young man who realizes that some problems in life—such as anti-Semitism or homophobia—cannot be dismissed with a laugh or a clever joke. Finally, in *Broadway Bound,* Eugene is portrayed as a grown man who has begun to recognize that comedy encompasses all of life—the good and the bad, the joy and the pain, the humor and the poignancy. Comedy should not only make people laugh, Eugene discovers; it should also make them "aware"—perhaps not politically aware, as his grandfather, Ben, would demand, but aware of life's absurdities, agonies, and possibilities. Comedy, Eugene has learned, must be real.

CHAPTER TEN

Lost in Yonkers

Simon's Pulitzer Prize-winning drama, *Lost in Yonkers* (1991), explores the issue of what happens when love is denied to human beings. Set in 1942 in Yonkers, New York, the play tells of two motherless Jewish boys—Jay, age fifteen, and Arty, age thirteen—who have come to live with their grandmother for ten months while their father earns the money to pay off his medical debts. Grandma Kurnitz, a refugee from Germany, is convinced that life brings nothing but pain and has dispensed with love and sentiment. Indeed, Grandma's four adult children have been scarred over the years by her coldness and abuse. Thirty-five-year-old Bella, who has a child's mentality, is especially starved for affection, and the grandsons themselves regard the old woman as ice cold and intimidating. Despite being a tender and amusing play, *Lost in Yonkers* is thus one of Simon's darker comedies—a portrait of a dysfunctional family.

Although it is not autobiographical in the manner of the Brighton Beach trilogy, the play still reflects some of Simon's personal history. When the father, Eddie, speaks in act 1 of his deceased wife's prolonged battle with cancer and of his efforts to give her the best possible medical care, Simon is undoubtedly recalling his own experience in coping with the illness of his first wife, Joan. Furthermore, the character of Eddie's gangster brother, Louie, was based on one of Simon's uncles, who worked as a bookkeeper for a Mafia-connected garment business and who one day mysteriously disappeared, presumably murdered by the mob. (Simon even initially thought about writing a play called "Louie the Gangster.")[1]

Grandma Kurnitz is modeled, at least slightly, on Simon's paternal grandmother, whom he saw only four or five times in his life. "She couldn't remember my name or my brother's," said the playwright. "I recall kissing her on the cheek, which was cold as ice. I didn't particularly like her."[2]

But the most important connection between *Lost in Yonkers* and Simon's own life has to do with the fear of being abandoned. During one of his father's many absences from the family, Simon and his mother moved in with relatives near Forest Hills, while Simon's brother, Danny, went to live with an aunt and uncle somewhere else. Like Jay and Arty in the play, Simon thus knew what it was like to be abandoned by his father and to be taken in by relatives. "It just seemed to me that dumping these two kids on the doorstep of this awful woman was a kind of wonderful Dickensian story. And yet I can say I know what it's like to be abandoned. It's one of the great fears of my life."[3]

Grandma Kurnitz's apartment, located directly above the soda fountain and candy store that she operates, sounds like an enticing home for a child. In reality, however, the Yonkers apartment is a kind of den of horrors. The principal horror is Grandma herself, who is portrayed not simply as a strict old woman but as a monster. Jay recalls being terribly afraid of his grandmother when he was younger, especially when she limped toward him with her cane and a murderous look in her eye. He tells his brother: "When I was five, I drew a picture of her and called it 'Frankenstein's Grandma.'"[4] One of the old woman's most dreadful features is her coldness. Arty remembers that he hated to kiss his grandmother: "It felt like putting your lips on a wrinkled ice cube" (90), he says. This iciness extends to Grandma Kurnitz's emotions as well. She is the only person who did not cry at the funeral of the boys' mother, and she is unsympathetic with Eddie's current financial plight, never offering to lend her son money (even though she has over ten thousand dollars hidden somewhere in the apartment) and refusing at first to allow Jay and Arty to live with her. All warmth, generosity, and motherly compassion have apparently been sapped from the woman.

More appalling than Grandma's coldness is her abuse of her own children. Jay claims that he heard of how Grandma used to hit Aunt Bella on the head with her cane whenever Bella did something foolish. If Bella mistakenly put the wrong number of scoops of ice cream in a soda, "Whacko! Another couple of I.Q. points gone" (91). The boys' Uncle Louie remembers how his mother would lock him in a closet if he broke a dish. "A ten-cent dish, I'd get two, three hours in the closet. And if I cried, I'd get another hour . . . No light, no water, just enough air to breathe. That's when I learned not to cry" (128). Grandma likewise abused Gert and Eddie, punishing them by withholding their supper for a week or striking them with her cane or hand. If Eddie sneaked treats from the candy store, Grandma would stare him down with eyes "like two district attorneys" until he broke down and confessed. Then "whack, he'd get that big German hand right across the head" (119).

Although Grandma Kurnitz doesn't physically abuse Jay and Arty, she frightens the boys and demonstrates that she has little interest in serving as their surrogate mother. In act 1, after she overhears Arty jokingly suggest that they cut off their grandmother's braids and sell them to the army for barbed wire, the old woman orders the boys to turn off the light and then threatens, "And you try cutting my braids off, you'll get your fingers chopped off" (112). In act 2 Grandma even fails to show compassion for Arty when he is sick, forcing him to eat some foul-tasting mustard soup and insisting that he get out of bed. "You lay in bed, you get fever. You get up und walk, da fever looks for somebody else. (SHE hits the bed with her cane twice.) Out! Out!" (125). When Arty complains that his mother used to let him stay in bed when he was sick, Grandma icily reminds him that he is no longer living in his mother's home.

Not surprisingly, Grandma Kurnitz has had a pernicious effect on the entire household. At the start of the play, Jay remarks to Arty, "Did you ever notice there's something wrong with *everyone* on Pop's side of the family?" (90). Aunt Gert, who no longer lives in the apartment, is reportedly so frightened of Grandma that she has developed a strange speech problem, uttering the first half of a sentence breathing out and the second half sucking in her breath. Uncle Louie has taken the toughness that Grandma ruthlessly pounded into him out into the streets, becoming a bagman for the mob. "It's like having a James Cagney movie in your own house" (122), quips Arty. And Eddie, until the time of his marriage to the boys' mother, was fearful and weak, never daring to challenge the iron rule of Grandma Kurnitz. "No, he was too afraid to go up against her," admits Louie. "He was careful. He never broke nothin' except maybe himself" (128).

But it is Aunt Bella who has been damaged most severely by her mother's callousness and abuse. Afflicted with scarlet fever as an infant, Bella did not talk until she was five years old, and when she finally began to communicate, her mother discouraged her from speaking very much. At age thirty-five, she is now emotionally arrested, or, as Jay puts it, her mind is "closed for repairs" (90). Bella gets confused easily, not even remembering that the boys' mother has died, and she literally gets lost when she ventures out of the

Yonkers apartment. At the start of the play, when Jay and Arty first observe Bella from the window, she inadvertently walks right past her home. Later, when the boys ask her what movie she has just seen, she answers, "I don't know. I couldn't find the theater I was looking for, so I went to the one I found" (94). Bella is "lost" not so much because of her mental disability but because her mother has withheld affection from her over the years, has physically abused her, and has encouraged her to remain childlike. "You vant to know vot you are, Bella?" says Grandma near the end of the play. "You're a child. Dot's vot da doctors told me. Not crazy. Not stupid . . . A child! And dot's how I treat you. Because dot's all you understand" (149).

In her essay "Beyond Laughter and Forgetting: Echoes of the Holocaust in Neil Simon's *Lost in Yonkers,*" Bette Mandl argues convincingly that the darker aspects of Jewish life in the 1940s subtly make their way into Simon's drama and that "the Holocaust casts its shadow on this work."[5] Nazism is not addressed directly in the play and is mentioned only briefly, as when Grandma tells Arty, "Und if you vere a boy growing up in Germany, you vould be dead by now" (126). But Grandma Kurnitz herself becomes emblematic of the terror associated with Nazism. With her erect bearing, her harsh authoritarian manner, and her heavy accent, she is pictured as more German than Jewish. At one point in the play, Louie even compares his mother to General Rommel, assuring Arty that although the Nazi general is tough, Grandma is tougher. "If Momma wanted him to eat the [mustard] soup, he would eat the soup" (127). According to Mandl, *Lost in Yonkers* resembles Arthur Miller's play *Broken Glass* (1994) in that "elements that recall the Nazis far away are superimposed on a Jewish figure at home, resulting in psychological havoc."⁶ Although a victim, Grandma Kurnitz has actually taken on the role of victimizer. Her intimidating presence is symbolically linked with fear, violence, and the distant terrors of the Holocaust. This explains, in a much broader sense, why she is truly "Frankenstein's Grandma."

At the end of act 1, Uncle Louie tells Jay and Arty that it is good to be home, adding, "There's nothing like family, boys. The one place in the world you're safe, is with your family" (123). Ironically, however, it is fear more than anything else that dominates this household in Yonkers. Everyone in the play is afraid of something —whether it is of Grandma, of loan sharks, or of the mysterious mobsters who are lurking in the background, threatening Uncle Louie's life. Interestingly enough, Grandma Kurnitz herself is not immune to the atmosphere of fear that pervades her home. In act 1, when the old woman refuses to let her grandsons move into the apartment, Bella is so desperate for companionship that she suddenly stands up to her mother, insisting that the boys be allowed to stay with them and threatening to move into a group care facility if Grandma doesn't change her mind. "And if I go, you'll be all alone . . . And you're afraid to be alone, Momma . . . Nobody else knows that but me" (110).

In coping with her fears, Grandma has adopted a ruthless philosophy, believing that people must be emotionally hardened if they are to survive in a cruel world. Having endured anti-Semitism in Germany, as well as the deaths of her husband and two children in America, Grandma is convinced that she must protect herself from life's pain by being hard and by teaching her children to be hard as well. "Dot's how I vas raised," she informs Eddie and his sons. "To be strong. Ven dey beat us vit sticks in Germany ven ve vere children,

I didn't cry . . . You don't survive in dis vorld vitout being like steel"
(108). Louie actually respects his mother for her ruthless strength.
He tells Arty that when Grandma was twelve years old, her foot was
crushed during a political rally in Berlin. She still suffers every day
from that injury, but Louie has never even seen his mother take an
aspirin. "She coulda had an operation but she used the money she
saved to get to this country with her husband and six kids. That's
moxie, kid" (128).

One of the play's chief ironies is that although Grandma has
imposed her severe will-to-live philosophy on her children, none of
them has actually turned out hard "like steel." Eddie, whose wife
taught him how to be loving and caring, is a devoted father to his
boys and a kind brother to Bella. Likewise, Gert is a warm and compassionate woman, someone who comforts Bella after a major confrontation with Grandma in act 2 and who offers her sister shelter in
her own home. Even Louie has a soft side. Though he talks tough
and carries a gun, he is really a gangster with a heart of gold. Louie
is protective of Bella, not wanting anyone (especially men) to take
advantage of his sister, and he is openly affectionate with Jay and
Arty, hugging the boys, giving them tips about how to deal with
their intimidating grandmother, and assuring them that their father is
a lucky man to have them.

But it is the child-like Bella whose warmth and capacity for love
contrasts most sharply with Grandma's steely coldness. Grandma
and Bella can be viewed as another of Simon's "odd couples"—
though not a humorous pair, by any means.[7] Whereas Grandma has
become emotionally deadened over the years, Bella still longs for
human contact and affection and, by some miracle, has retained her
softness and her ability to be tender; indeed, Bella, rather than

Grandma, actually provides the nurturing influence that her mother-less nephews need in the Yonkers apartment. Because Grandma and Bella are presented as opposites, it is inevitable that the two women should clash during the course of the drama—especially in act 2, when Bella announces to the family that she has met a man whom she plans to marry—a theater usher named Johnny, who is mentally handicapped. Bella wants to be this man's wife, have his children, and open a restaurant with him, a business that she hopes her mother will support financially.

The scene in which Bella makes her important announcement to the family demonstrates Simon's special gift for combining comedy with tragedy. Initially Bella behaves in a humorous, childlike manner, fussing about where people will sit during her announcement and sulking when Louie decides to stand. Once Bella recognizes Louie and Grandma's resistance to her marriage plans, however, she delivers a poignant monologue in which she argues that she will be a good wife and mother and that she will give her babies all the love that Grandma denied to her own children. "Let me have my babies, Momma," she pleads. "Because I have to love somebody. I have to love someone who'll love me back before I die" (145). Within minutes during this scene Simon actually takes his audience from laughter to tears—a feat that critic William A. Henry III applauded in his review of the play for *Time:* "The ability to find humor in unlikely places, then shift emotional gears with no machinery showing, makes Simon a great comedist."[8]

Caught in the middle of these family conflicts, Jay and Arty provide *Lost in Yonkers* with its comic perspective, serving throughout the play as a kind of amusing Greek chorus. But to a certain extent the boys are developed as characters in their own right and are more than mere wisecracking commentators. During their ten-month stay in Grandma Kurnitz's home, Jay and Arty not only survive, they grow stronger. Arty demonstrates his "moxie," as Uncle Louie calls it, when he scolds Grandma for treating him so harshly during his illness. If someone made her miserable in Germany, he says, she should "take it out on Hitler, not on [him]" (126). Similarly, Jay shows newfound strength when he defends his father in front of Uncle Louie, arguing that Eddie may not be as tough as Louie but that at least he is doing something for the war effort, selling scrap iron to make tanks and ships. "What are *you* doing?" Jay demands. "Hiding in your mother's apartment and scaring little kids and acting like Humphrey Bogart. Well, you're no Humphrey Bogart" (136). After this speech, Louie smiles and says, "You know what you got, Jay? You got moxie" (136).

Not only do Jay and Arty grow stronger during their stay with their grandmother, but they also have a positive effect on her dysfunctional family. Whereas Grandma and her adult children are plagued by emotional and personal problems, Jay and Arty are reasonably well adjusted. They are typical boys who enjoy playing sports, eating ice cream, and going to Yankees games. Jay and Arty represent normalcy, and indeed, the two of them bring a much-needed element of normalcy into Grandma Kurnitz's Yonkers apartment. It can be argued, in fact, that by the end of the boys' visit, this dysfunctional family has changed, to some extent, and their behavior has become more "normal." The monstrous Grandma Kurnitz softens slightly, even allowing Eddie and the boys to kiss her goodbye; Louie abandons his mobster activities in New York in order to join the army, telling the boys beforehand, "maybe one day you'll be proud of your old Uncle Louie" (136); and Bella, though still living with Grandma after Johnny decides not to go through with their marriage plans, claims that from now on she wants to make new friends and lead as normal an adult life as possible. Although Jay and Arty have not deliberately tried to solve the problems that beset this household, their prolonged visit has seemingly changed the family for the better.

According to Paul H. Grawe, "Comedy's basic message is that the human race will survive, that it is destined to carry on."[9] This hopeful message is communicated in most of Simon's plays—from his Menandrian comedies, in which the renewal of a marriage suggests growth and fecundity, to his darker comedies (e.g., *The Prisoner of Second Avenue*) in which the protagonists adopt a kind of survival mentality in order to cope with contemporary urban life. In *Lost in Yonkers* Jay conveys this message of survival near the end of the play when he exclaims, "We made it, Arty. Ten months here and we're still alive. We got through Grandma and we're all right" (153). The boys manage to survive their ordeal in Yonkers not only because of their own inner strength, or "moxie," but because during the ten months at their grandmother's house they have continued to be loved—by Bella, by Louie, by their absent father, even by Gert. Miraculously enough, all of the characters who have suffered from Grandma's abuse are, at the end of the play, still capable of love and compassion.

In presenting this comedy of survival, Simon makes significant use of voice-overs—a relatively new dramatic device for him. In previous plays, such as *The Prisoner of Second Avenue, The Sunshine Boys,* and *Broadway Bound,* Simon included the voice of an unseen radio or television announcer, but this is the first play in which he uses the kind of voice-overs that one typically associates with film. Not only do the voice-overs create a bridge between scenes and indicate the passage of time, but they also allow Simon to keep the character of Eddie in the play, even when Eddie is on his travels in the South. The voice-overs (mostly letters from Eddie to his sons) reveal the father's struggles, his health problems, and above all, his devotion to his two boys. When Eddie has to take a week off from his work to rest, he writes to say, "Nothing to worry about. I'll be on the road again real soon and I promise I'll make up the time" (112).

Another important function of the voice-overs is that they provide the play with comic relief. Eddie's accounts of his life as a New York Jew traveling in the South are laced with humor, revealing that he is entirely out of his element in this culture. Eddie complains about Southern food, saying, "I haven't eaten anything down here that wasn't fried, smoked, hashed, gritted or poned . . . or wasn't caught in a swamp, a tree, or coming out of a hole in the ground" (110), and he admits that a woman didn't understand him when he used the term "Sho nuff." In act 2 Simon also places voice-overs directly after several of his most emotional scenes in order to offer comic relief. After a highly emotional exchange between Bella and Grandma near the end of the play, for example, Bella writes a postcard to Eddie with the message: "I just want to tell you that Arty and Jay are all right and I have good news for you except I don't have no more room. Love, Bella" (153).

As Northrop Frye points out in *Anatomy of Criticism,* comedy tends to move toward the creation of a new society, one that serves as a sort of moral norm and that includes as many individuals as possible in its final community. The villains, or the obstructing characters, Frye writes, "are more often reconciled or converted than simply repudiated."[10] In keeping with this classical tradition, *Lost in*

Yonkers moves toward the creation of a new society which, in Simon's comedy, is simply a healthier family structure. By the end of the play, Grandma (the obstructing character) is converted slightly, relinquishing some of her iron control and managing to reconcile— at least as much as it is possible for her to do so—with Bella, Eddie, and her grandsons. The old woman begins to communicate more openly with Bella, offers grudging praise to Eddie for settling his massive debt on his own, and hints that in the future, she would enjoy seeing her grandsons more often.

The creation of this new society can also be viewed as a movement from tyranny to freedom. As Frye observes, the plots of many of Shakespeare's comedies begin with "some absurd, cruel, or irrational law . . . which the action of the comedy then evades or breaks."[11] In *Lost in Yonkers* the representative of that cruel law is Grandma Kurnitz herself, whose tyranny is even compared to the horrors of Nazism. By the end of the play the other characters are freer from Grandma's despotic rule, not only because they have left her home (as have Jay and Arty) or because they have gathered the courage to stand up to her (as has Bella) but also because Grandma herself is somewhat willing to modify the nature of her authority. Like many classical comedies, then, *Lost in Yonkers* delineates what Frye calls a movement "from a society controlled by habit, ritual bondage, arbitrary law and the older characters to a society controlled by youth and pragmatic freedom."[12]

Despite its comic resolution, however, Simon's ending is not "candy colored," as critic Clive Barnes suggested in an otherwise positive review of the play.[13] Grandma is still stern and aloof, admonishing the boys not to play games in the house ("If dey break someting, dey'll pay plenty" [154], she warns Eddie) and dismissing

Eddie's suggestion that Jay and Arty bid her good-bye: "Ve said goodbye dis morning. Two goodbyes is too much" (154). Furthermore, with the boys gone, Bella will undoubtedly remain "lost" in Yonkers, especially since she must continue to live with her cold and demanding mother. We have no idea if Bella will ever find someone to love her in the way she dreams or if she will have the babies that she so desperately wants. Simon thus brings some light into this dark comedy by the time the final curtain falls, but by deliberately preserving the play's realism, he avoids a "candy-colored" ending—even in a drama that is set above "Kurnitz's Kandy Store" (89).

In 1991 *Lost in Yonkers* received both the Tony Award for Best Play and the Pulitzer Prize for drama. Simon had previously won the Tony Award for Best Play for *Biloxi Blues* (1985) and was also the recipient of the New York Drama Critics Circle Award for *Brighton Beach Memoirs* (1983), but the Pulitzer Prize had always eluded him. (In fact, Simon assumed that in 1991 the award would go to John Guare for *Six Degrees of Separation*.) Informing the Pulitzer Advisory Board of the drama jury's decision, Douglas Watt wrote that *Lost in Yonkers* was the only play nominated by all five jurors, who viewed it as "a mature work by an enduring (and often undervalued) American playwright."[14] Simon himself was deeply gratified by the award. "I never think of the prizes I may or may not get, especially the Pulitzer," he remarked. "But when I got it, it was like climbing a mountain that I always wanted to climb, and I was glad that I got there."[15] Indeed, for almost three decades Neil Simon had been perceived by critics as a popular and highly entertaining playwright. Now, at long last, America's master of comedy was being honored as a serious dramatist.

CHAPTER ELEVEN

Jake's Women and *Laughter on the 23rd Floor*

Jake's Women

"The Inside of His Head"—Arthur Miller's original title for *Death of a Salesman*—might be a fitting description of Simon's next play, *Jake's Women* (1992), a work that opened in San Diego in 1990 but that required major revisions before making its Broadway debut two years later. Departing from the conventions of the realistic theater, *Jake's Women* is an expressionistic drama focusing on the inner world of a middle-aged writer—a man who is especially dependent on the women in his life: his sister, his deceased wife, his current wife, his daughter, and his psychoanalyst. Through a Pirandellian blend of present-day reality, flashbacks, and imagined conversations, Simon portrays Jake as someone who is consumed by his work, who is emotionally isolated, and who is so busy observing life that he frequently fails to participate in it. It is the writer's search for human connection, therefore, which becomes the play's principal subject.

Simon's expressionistic approach is made clear in the opening stage directions, which reveal that the drama "takes place both in Jake's apartment and in his mind. The apartment is minimal, his mind is overflowing. There are no walls, no windows, no sense of place and even time is indefinite."[1] As Jake sits in his upstairs office, which is spartanly furnished with a desk, chair, and word processor, he imagines people who "seemingly appear from nowhere and leave the same way" (159). These are the women in his life—the people who have meant the most to him, including his first wife, Julie, who died in an automobile accident ten years earlier. During the course of the play, Jake is occasionally interrupted by real-life events—a telephone call from his sister or the arrival home of his wife, Maggie. For much of the drama, however, the audience is inside the mind of the writer, moving between the present and the past, between fact and fantasy. As critic Jack Kroll observed, Simon "[mixes] time periods and states of mind in an often brilliant crossfire of confrontations."[2]

Another expressionistic feature of *Jake's Women* is that the protagonist breaks through the imaginary "fourth wall" onstage and speaks directly to the audience. Like Eugene Jerome in the Brighton Beach trilogy, Jake introduces the other characters and comments upon them, sometimes in a humorous fashion. He explains, for example, that his sister, Karen, who attended film school at New York University, "made a three-hour student film of *her,* just sitting on a kitchen chair, called *Loneliness*" (163). Like Eugene Jerome, Jake also addresses the audience in order to reveal his innermost thoughts and to make some sort of connection with others. He suggests that "we're all writers in a sense" (163)—that we all create imaginary scenes and conversations: "There's not one of you who hasn't thought . . . of what it would be like to talk to your father who died five or twenty years ago. Would he look the same? Would you still be his little girl? . . . Or the boy you loved in college who married someone else. What would your life be if he proposed to you instead? . . . You've played that scene out. We *all* do it" (218).

Despite its experimental approach, *Jake's Women* makes use of the traditional "problem marriage" framework, derived from

Menandrian New Comedy, which Simon employed in many of his previous dramas. When the play begins, Jake admits that his eight-year marriage to Maggie is in trouble. Both he and Maggie have been unfaithful, and both are so absorbed in their work (Jake in his writing and Maggie in her business career) that they have grown apart. Feeling isolated and unloved, Maggie believes that Jake's first wife, Julie, still comes between them and that "Jake the writer" especially gets in the way of their relationship—the man who is so consumed with inventing his own characters and living in their world that he causes her to feel like "a rewrite of someone else" (181).

Yet rather than dealing with these obstacles, Jake retreats even further into his writer's imagination, calling up pleasant memories from his past (such as the first time that he met Maggie) or inventing conversations with the people who are closest to him. He summons up the image of his sister, Karen, because he realizes that she will be sympathetic and supportive, and of his daughter, Molly, because he knows that she will tell him that she loves him. In an additional effort to comfort himself, Jake evokes the image of his deceased wife, Julie, a woman who is still extremely dear to him and who understands his weakness and dependency. "Now I see why you bring me back," Julie tells him. "It's mostly when you're in trouble, isn't it?" (185).

Throughout the play Jake uses his imagination not only to comfort himself but also to analyze himself, to punish himself, and to lay bare his own inadequacies. During his initial conversation with his sister, Karen, for instance, Jake turns to the audience and remarks that the interesting question is "not 'Why is Karen irritating me now?' but why am I making her irritate me?" (164). He creates an imaginary scene in which Karen speaks harshly to him about his infidelity to Maggie, deliberately reviving his feelings of guilt. Similarly, when Jake summons up the image of his psychoanalyst, Edith, he pictures her as a sassy woman who speaks to him as if he were an infant and who bluntly tells him that his life is in his own hands. "You're unhappy if you want to be. You're lonely if you want to be. It's your choice" (177).

In "*Jake's Women:* A Dialogue," Brian Rhinehart persuasively argues that the audience in Simon's play not only becomes privy to Jake's emotional problems but in a sense also takes on the role of analyst: "By making the audience an observer of Jake's psychic processes, Simon . . . open[s] up a kind of transferential dialogue between the individual audience member and the performance. It's not surprising that Simon enjoys the moniker 'Doc Simon.' He seems to know that people benefit from his art, just as an analyst benefits, through processes of transference, from a dialogue with a patient."[3] Witnessing Jake's psychological turmoil, the audience (as analyst) becomes aware that many of the protagonist's problems are related to his profession as a writer. Simon briefly addressed some of these problems in earlier plays such as *The Good Doctor, Chapter Two,* and the Brighton Beach trilogy. But *Jake's Women* is his most self-reflexive drama because it actually pulls the audience into the mind of the writer and offers, as Clive Barnes notes, a "bizarrely convincing portrait of the artist as a hall of mirrors."[4]

That portrait reveals a man who desperately needs control in his life and who enjoys the sense of omnipotence that his writing affords him. Pointing to his office, Jake tells the audience, "That little room up there is eight by ten feet but to me it's the world. The universe! You don't get to play God, you get to *be* God!" (163). In real life, however, the protagonist enjoys no such feelings of control.

During his first imaginary conversation with Maggie, she reminds Jake that he is not all-powerful, claiming that she knows he is afraid "because you can never control what I say when reality begins" (162). In act 2, after Jake has been separated from Maggie for six months, he even begins to lose control of the figures who appear in his imagination. He tells the audience: "No longer did I summon up the Karens and Ediths and Mollys of my life to help brighten up the endless sleepless nights . . . Now they came on their own. Uninvited. Unsummoned. Unstoppable" (198). Jake's professional life is out of control (he can't seem to write anything worth keeping), and his personal life is in shambles. "I do feel like I'm losing a grip on myself," he confesses. "As if I'm spiraling down in diminishing circles like water being drained from a bathtub, and suddenly my big toe is being sucked down into the hole and I'm screaming for my life . . . No. Not my life. My mother" (202).

Jake also suffers from his alienation as an artist. Completely absorbed in his writing, the protagonist worries about missing out on real life. He can spend eight hours in his office writing words that will be captured permanently on the page, but, as he reminds the audience, "the eight hours of your life is gone and you'll never see those again, brother" (163). In act 2, when Jake imagines a tender reunion between his deceased wife, Julie, and their now grown-up daughter, Molly, he is especially struck by his artistic detachment, asking himself: "If I can create *this* intimacy, why can't I experience it in my own life?" (217–18).

Despite his emotional isolation, Jake makes it clear that he writes because he needs to write and because writing gives him the only security that he has ever known. "I write to survive," he explains to Maggie near the end of the play. "It's the only thing that doesn't reject me. My characters are the only ones I know who love me unconditionally, because I give them life" (224–25). Jake thus views his occupation as both a curse and a blessing—a natural calling from which he can never really escape. Like the Chekhovian figure of the Writer in *The Good Doctor,* Jake might well have explained his endless compulsion to produce page after page and story after story by simply saying, "I have no choice. I am a writer."[5]

A reviewer for *Time* called *Jake's Women* "Neil Simon's most nakedly autobiographical play," not so much because this experimental drama makes use of events in the author's own life (such as the death of his first wife, Joan, and the breakup of his marriage to his second wife, Marsha Mason) but because the play offers an "acidly self-critical" portrait of the writer himself.[6] In fact, Simon has often described himself as someone who, like Jake, feels compelled to write: "I don't think I'll ever give up writing because if I tried, I couldn't," Simon once told a group of fellow playwrights. "When I walk past my study it pulls me in like a magnet, and there I am."[7] Marsha Mason, speaking of her ex-husband's work as a playwright, also confirmed Simon's resemblance to Jake by remarking, "A lot of it has to do with having control. That's very important to Neil, because it gives him a sense of security and solidarity."[8] Furthermore, Simon has himself admitted to being a "voyeur" like Jake—someone who is "constantly observing rather than participating" in life.[9] Indeed, Diane Lander, Simon's third wife, actually made it a condition of the couple's pre-nuptial agreement that her husband never write about her or her daughter during Diane's lifetime. As she explained, she wanted Simon to live the relationship rather than use it as raw material for his plays.[10]

In *Jake's Women* the protagonist/writer wishes to reconnect with the real world by salvaging his marriage, but first he must come to terms with two women from his past who serve as obstacles to that union: his deceased wife and his mother. Jake's imaginary conversation with Julie in act 2 (including her reunion with their daughter) represents a genuine effort on the protagonist's part to let go of his first wife. Not only does the imaginary Julie encourage Jake to save his present marriage, but she even cautions him not to idealize her so much in the future: "I don't want to be a shrine. I don't want to be a touched-up photo in a family album" (214). Although Jake's mother never actually appears in the play, the protagonist clearly connects her with some of his deepest fears: (1) his fear of abandonment (when he was five he awoke from a nap to discover that his mother was gone); (2) his fear of being controlled (she used to tie him into his high chair with a rope); and (3) according to Brian Rhinehart, even his fear of castration (revealed in the fantasy about his toe being sucked down the drain). Near the end of the play, however, when Jake hears a voice saying, "I love you . . . and I forgive you" (227), he realizes, with some amazement, that it is his own voice and that he himself must say these words to his mother if he is to bridge "those last two inches" (229) that seem to separate him from Maggie.

Jake's Women concludes with the renewal of the protagonist's marriage—an ending that is in keeping with the Menandrian framework of Simon's play and that also accentuates Jake's process of self-discovery. When the real-life Maggie returns to Jake's apartment, willing to work out the couple's differences, Jake finally recognizes that he wants to emerge from his writer's hideaway and join his wife in the real world—a step that is extremely difficult for him to take. "It's a ten-mile drop from here to there" (229), he nervously tells her, speaking from the top of the stairs to his office. As the play ends, Jake and Maggie reach for each other on the stairs, "like God and Adam reaching out in the Sistine Chapel" (229)—a tableau that refers back to Jake's sense of omnipotence as a writer but that, as Brian Rhinehart notes, also "elevates Jake and Maggie's 're-connection' on the stairs to the level of religious epiphany."[11] Although this ending might strike some playgoers as far-fetched, it is consistent not only with the expressionistic style of the drama but also with Simon's fundamental view of love as life-giving and redemptive. Moreover, the final tableau is appropriate because it emphasizes the effort, the actual *reaching* that has to be done, if Jake, Maggie, or any human being is to make this sacred connection.

Laughter on the 23rd Floor

Whereas *Jake's Women* explores the private world of a solitary writer, *Laughter on the 23rd Floor* (1993) examines the public, communal world of television comedy writing. Set in 1953, the play is based on Simon's own experience as a writer for Sid Caesar's legendary *Your Show of Shows* during television's Golden Age of Comedy. According to Simon, working on the show was one of the most exhilarating experiences of his life because he was surrounded by some of the world's funniest people, including Sid Caesar, Carl Reiner, Mel Brooks, and Larry Gelbart.[12] *Laughter on the 23rd Floor* is an affectionate salute to these gifted writers and comedians, much as *The Sunshine Boys* is a tribute to the lost art of vaudeville. But the play's central theme has to do with the importance of community. Indeed, the writers are pictured not so much as individuals but as co-workers, teammates—even a family. As their eccentric leader and star, Max Prince, assures them, "My writers are my flesh and blood."[13]

The comedy takes place in the Writers' Room for *The Max Prince Show*—a setting which, like Jake's office in *Jake's Women,* is a kind of universe unto itself. Located in New York on the twenty-third floor of a building on Fifty-seventh Street, the Writers' Room brings together seven writers who meet daily to share funny stories, trade one-liners, and come up with ideas for their weekly variety show. Theirs is a fractious, zany, joke-filled world that is predominantly Jewish and almost exclusively male. Carol Wyman, the only female on the staff, even claims that she has been masculinized by her experience in the Writers' Room, picking up coarse language from the other men and returning home smelling like cigar smoke. She says that she cannot survive there as a woman: "I don't want to be called a woman writer. I want to be called a *good* writer, and if it means being one of the guys then I'll be one of the guys" (286). The Writers' Room is thus a masculine haven—a home of sorts—but it is also a place where tensions, fears, and hostilities come to the fore-front. As critic Jeremy Gerard noted, the room is "equal parts pressure cooker, sanctuary, and war zone."[14]

Lucas Brickman, a shy young man who is a newcomer to the Writers' Room, serves as the play's narrator and comic *raisonneur.* Based on Simon himself, Lucas provides an outsider's perspective on Max Prince and his comedy team, breaking through the "fourth wall" onstage and addressing the audience directly. Yet unlike Jake in *Jake's Women* or Eugene Jerome in the Brighton Beach trilogy, Lucas actually reveals very little of himself during the course of the play. Rather than spotlighting Lucas (and thus creating an autobiographical allegory), Simon is more interested in developing a group portrait. His real subject is male bonding and the forming of a community—or what Linda Winer has called the "manic camaraderie" among the writers in the Writers' Room.[15]

In sketching this group portrait, Simon (through Lucas) accentuates the writers' personal eccentricities. Milt Fields, for instance, dresses in a funny costume or hat each day in order to get attention. "When I walk in here, Max Prince laughs," he says. "And if Max Prince laughs, my kids eat this week" (235). Val Skolsky, a Russian immigrant, is inclined to comment wryly on the American dream. Picking up a bagel, he says: "Look at this. Already sliced. *This* is why my father brought us to America" (237). Lucas also introduces the audience to Brian Doyle, a heavy-smoking, heavy-drinking Irishman; to Kenny Franks, a genius joke-maker; to Carol Wyman, a feisty career woman who tries to hold her own with the men; and to Ira Stone, a serious hypochondriac whose "greatest wish in life [is] to have a virus named after him" (247). Realizing that he is joining a community of eccentrics, Lucas remarks: "I knew then and there that if I was going to keep my job, I'd have to become as totally crazy as the rest of them" (265).

Although the writers themselves are eccentric, they primarily serve as reflector characters for the show's outlandish star, Max Prince (modeled on Sid Caesar)—a man who displays both comic genius and emotional unbalance. Skillfully building an entrance for Max (much as he did for Felix Ungar in *The Odd Couple*), Simon makes it clear in act 1 that the man is paranoid, wildly eccentric, and on the verge of a nervous breakdown. The writers speak of how Max, despite his enormous talent, is exceedingly nervous performing a live program every week. "Max likes it in here, with us," says Val, "not out there. The funniest man since Chaplin and he still throws up before every show" (243). According to Kenny Franks, Max even claimed that he had received a threatening letter the previous night and that after taking one of his "scotch-tranquilizer combos," he had sat at home "with a loaded shotgun on his lap" (246), waiting for the enemy.

So paranoid is Max that he interprets NBC's current plan to reduce both the budget and airtime of his variety show as a McCarthyist attack—a threat to artistic freedom. The network is responding to an expanding television audience that wants to watch quiz shows, wrestling, bowling, and comedies like *Father Knows Best.* But Max connects NBC's decisions with the blacklisting and political witch-hunts that are currently taking place in America as a whole. When informed that Sen. Joseph McCarthy has just accused five-star general George Marshall of being a Communist, an enraged Max punches his fist through a wall, declaring that he wants the hole framed in Tiffany's best silver, with a gold plaque underneath containing the engraved words: "'In honor of General George Marshall, Soldier, Statesman, Slandered by that son of a bitch McCarthy'" (257).

Max himself adopts the role of the military braggart, a stock character seen throughout the history of comedy—from Aristophanes' *The Acharnians* to Charlie Chaplin's *Great Dictator.*[16] For Max the announcement of cutbacks by NBC represents not only a McCarthyist threat but also a declaration of war. Indeed, the comedy star pictures himself as the intrepid military commander who must lead his troops through the present crisis. "NBC fired the first shot," he tells the writers. "Remember this day, everyone. A day that will live in infamy. . . . The battle has started. The lines have been drawn. Now we have to plan our counterattack" (250). Inflating his martial rhetoric further, Max announces that the time for diplomacy with the network is over and that blood will be spilled. "But not in my house. Their palaces will crumble and their kings will fall and their wheat fields will be scorched" (252). Such bombastic rhetoric makes Max's defiance laughable, to be sure, but it also draws the television star and his writers closer together, like fellow soldiers in an actual war. United against a common enemy (NBC), the seven writers and Max form a military unit, as it were—a genuine brotherhood, a family.

In recounting the antics of Max Prince and his team of comedy writers, Simon largely dispenses with plot (much to the chagrin of critics like Clive Barnes, who claimed that in *Laughter on the 23rd Floor* Simon had written a string of one-liners instead of a drama).[17] But the play does have a fundamental structure—one that might be described by the musical term "riffing" or by the phrase "miscellaneous bits."[18] Basically, Simon presents a series of jokes and gags that revolve around a central situation—the threat to *The Max Prince Show* from NBC. Although Simon had been criticized in the past for the overuse of gags and one-liners, in *Laughter on the 23rd Floor* virtually all of the characters are comedy writers, so the jokes are more easily justified. As Michael Feingold noted in his review, "The one thing Simon has always done brilliantly is construct gags. Here nothing stands in his way: Each entrance is a gag, each costume change a gag, each character trait a running gag, each dispute a routine."[19] When Brian Doyle arrives late at the Writers' Room, for instance, he says: "I'm sorry. I just stopped to—(HE coughs.) I stopped to—(HE coughs again, almost uncontrollably, then stops.) I stopped to get some cigarettes" (239). Likewise, when Ira Stone finally appears at the office, the running gag about his hypochondria

Laughter and Tears

fared well with the critics. Even Aristotle,
d comedy as a lesser genre: "Poetry now
ns, according to the individual character of
pirits imitated noble action and the actions
ragedy]. The more trivial sort imitated the
ns [satire and comedy]." Aristotle added:
through which Tragedy passed, and the
are well known, whereas Comedy has had
not first treated seriously."¹ Indeed, it can
still not treated seriously by many schol-
e case of Neil Simon, the most successful
y in the twentieth century. Simon's plays
for more than thirty-five years, but they
by critics as lighthearted entertainment.
ce, in a general editor's note to Gary
usebook (1997), writes: "Although he is
would probably not wish to become one,
e most famous and most commercially
merica."² Like many critics, King appar-
does not qualify as serious literature—or
Neil Simon, which, in King's view, are
pular culture. To be sure, there has been
rest in Simon's plays ever since the
e for drama in 1991. Yet one remains
holarly criticism that has been devoted

---

begins: "I can't breathe. I can't catch my breath. I think it's a heart
attack. It could be a stroke. Don't panic, just do what I tell you"
(260).

Just as Willie Clark and Al Lewis in *The Sunshine Boys* con-
nect with each other through an exchange of jokes and one-liners,
so, too, do the writers in the Writers' Room. These people communicate with each other almost exclusively through a series of funny
stories, gags, insults, and wisecracks; and in so doing, they form a
community of comics. The excellence of their teamwork is made
clear during a scene in act 2, in which the writers are working on a
comedy sketch that spoofs the new film version of *Julius Caesar*.
Not only do the writers skillfully parody Shakespearean English
(e.g., "What news from Flavius and Lepidus?. . . . Not well. Flavius
has mucus and Lepidus is nauseous" [281]), but they also lampoon
Marlon Brando's performance in the film:[20]

Kenny   What dost thou seekest in the constellations, Caesar?
Max   (Reads, doing Brando.) A clustuh a stahs in da
        heavens.
Brian   And by what name dost this cluster be called,
        oh, Caesar?
Max   It is called Stelluh . . . *Stelluh!* . . . Stelluh
        for Stahlight!

                                                    (283)

The Julius Caesar sketch functions as a play-within-the-play
of sorts, much like Willie Clark and Al Lewis's vaudeville
sketch in *The Sunshine Boys*. It provides a view of the writers
engaged in their actual craft, revealing their collective talent and
their effectiveness when working as a team. Furthermore, this

sketch about the death of Caesar is particularly appropriate for a play that describes the demise of Sid Caesar's legendary comedy show. The line "Caesar reigns no more" (286), in fact, carries a significant double meaning.

In *Laughter on the 23rd Floor* Simon deviates from the traditional comedic happy ending, focusing on the painful breakup of a tight-knit community rather than on the restoration of social harmony. Unable to face his staff with the truth about the cancellation of *The Max Prince Show,* a drunken Max informs the writers that they have actually won the war, that NBC has surrendered, and that they have all gotten what they really wanted: their independence from the network. "We beat the bastards," he insists, "and we beat them together" (294). Before making his final exit, Max also tells the writers that he loves them—something he confesses he never said in his own family. The demise of *The Max Prince Show* is equally hard on the writers, who love their work and who are accustomed to functioning together as a team. "To be honest, we were all a little frightened," admits Lucas. "Because until now, we all had each other to lean on. But like little chicks leaving the nest, we'd soon know the fear, the panic and the courage needed to fly by ourselves" (287).

Laughter on the 23rd Floor, as its title suggests, is ultimately about laughter itself and the special way that laughter can bring people together. Max Prince and his comedy writers have formed a unique community in the Writers' Room—a family that is nourished and supported through the laughter that the characters themselves create. When the show is first threatened with cutbacks, Kenny even argues that Max and the writers should make an effort to stick together and continue their work, "because maybe we'll never have

to Simon's comedies throughout his career. As Walter Kerr once remarked, "Whenever a playwright manages to be hilariously funny all night long . . . he is in immediate danger of being condescended to."[3]

Among Simon's many play scripts, there are, of course, some notable disappointments—for example, *The Star-Spangled Girl* (1966), a play that Simon admits he should not have written at all; *God's Favorite* (1974), an unsuccessful modern rendering of the Book of Job; and the more recent *London Suite* (1995), a group of one-act plays that is inferior to its predecessors, *Plaza Suite* and *California Suite*. But Simon has also created a number of outstanding plays, demonstrating that he is an accomplished and versatile dramatist. He has proven himself to be a master of light romantic comedy (as in *Barefoot in the Park*), of farce (as in the last act of *Plaza Suite*), and of high comedy (as in the "Visitors from London" portion of *California Suite*). *The Sunshine Boys* is a humorous, poignant, and skillfully crafted play, as is *Broadway Bound*—a work that some critics viewed as the best play of the 1980s. *The Odd Couple*, despite its third-act problems, is already a classic of the American stage; and *Lost in Yonkers*, for which Simon won the Pulitzer Prize, represents the author at his comedic best.

Simon's willingness to experiment with his dramatic craft should also not go unnoticed. During his lengthy career Simon has repeatedly taken risks and has deliberately moved in new directions. This willingness to experiment can be seen in works such as *The Gingerbread Lady*, in which Simon attempts to combine comedy with tragedy; in *The Good Doctor*, in which he offers a pastiche of sketches based on the short stories of Chekhov; and in *Fools* (1981), a fairy tale-like romance patterned after *Fiddler on the Roof* and the stories of Sholem Aleichem. In *Rumors* (1988) Simon decided to write a full-length farce for the first time in his career, well aware of the challenges that the form presents—particularly the need for fast-paced action, surprising twists, and continuous humor. He experimented with dramatic narration not only in the Brighton Beach trilogy but also in *Jake's Women,* which takes place primarily in the mind of the protagonist, and in *Proposals* (1998), in which the story is recounted by the ghost of an African-American housekeeper. Such experimental efforts have sometimes failed to gain popular or critical acclaim, but they demonstrate Simon's seriousness as a playwright and his interest in breaking new ground.

Why have Neil Simon's comedies enjoyed so much popularity over the years? First of all, Simon has consistently given his audiences the gift of laughter—no small accomplishment in itself. His plays are often brilliantly funny, revealing the author's talent for both situational and verbal humor. Simon's flair for rapid-fire jokes and wisecracks is unparalleled. Second, during a period of drastic cultural change, audiences have appreciated Simon's adherence to traditional values, specifically those relating to marriage and the family unit. Neither didactic nor politically motivated, Simon has nonetheless served as a spokesman for the "silent majority," voicing the values and fears not only of contemporary New Yorkers but of Middle America as a whole. Playgoers have responded to Simon because they see themselves in the author's characters—everyday people who are fallible and insecure, yet who, like Barney Cashman in *Last of the Red Hot Lovers,* are basically "decent, loving, gentle human beings" (646). Finally, Simon's comedies are appealing because they strike audiences as representations of real life. Indeed, the playwright's most important contribution to the American theater

BETWEEN LAUGHTER AND TEARS

may be the development of a realistic, bittersweet sort of comedy in which humor and sadness are inextricably intertwined. Simon's comic terrain, as one critic has aptly noted, is always "the border country between laughter and tears."[4]

Movie Adaptations of Simon's Plays

Neil Simon passed up the opportunity to write the movie script for his first comedy, *Come Blow Your Horn,* preferring to devote his attention to playwriting. But, disappointed with the 1963 Paramount production, Simon made an effort thereafter to control his material and to write the screenplays for his own comedies. As Robert K. Johnson has noted, Simon's movie adaptations are sometimes overly faithful to the originals, becoming little more than photographed plays.[1] Simon himself has admitted to this tendency, particularly in the movie scripts for some of his early plays such as *Plaza Suite, Last of the Red Hot Lovers,* and *The Prisoner of Second Avenue.* "I really didn't have an interest in films then," explained Simon. "I was mainly interested in continuing writing for the theater. . . . The plays never became cinematic."[2]

The Odd Couple (Paramount, 1968), featuring Walter Matthau and Jack Lemmon, is an example of a highly successful early adaptation—one that is faithful to the dramatic version but is "opened up" photographically so that it seems less like a filmed play. Unlike the original comedy, the movie begins with a scene in which a despondent Felix checks into a cheap hotel then bungles his attempt to jump from his ninth-floor window. The screenplay thus does not endeavor to "build an entrance" for Felix, as was done so adroitly in the Broadway version.

The Sunshine Boys (MGM, 1975), another of Simon's most effective adaptations, showcases the talents of Walter Matthau and

George Burns. Simon changes locations and adds several new episodes to the movie (e.g., Willie's unsuccessful audition for a potato chip commercial), but he transfers most of the original play to the screen intact. In a 1997 remake of the *The Sunshine Boys* for television, Simon altered his play script substantially—updating the dialogue; substituting a niece (Nancy) for Willie's nephew, Ben; eliminating the vaudeville sketch; and turning Al Lewis (played by Woody Allen) into a more voluble and acerbic character. The television version lacks the energy and charm, however, of the 1975 movie.

By the time Simon worked on the movie script for *California Suite* (Columbia, 1978), his interest in writing screenplays had increased (in part because of the influence of his second wife, actress Marsha Mason), and he was more willing to experiment with his material. Instead of presenting four separate one-acts, as he had on Broadway, Simon smoothly intercut the stories so that they occurred contemporaneously, creating the sense of a single, cohesive comedy. He also "opened up" the sketches, shifting locations to include scenes outside the Beverly Hills Hotel.

Only When I Laugh (Columbia, 1981) is notable among Simon's movie adaptations in that it is radically changed from the play upon which it is based, employing less than half of the material from the script of *The Gingerbread Lady*.[3] The ex-nightclub singer Evy Meara becomes Georgia Hines—a divorced actress who is battling alcoholism as she struggles to establish a closer relationship with her teenage daughter, Polly. Unlike Evy, however, Georgia is not a nymphomaniac; she has a genuine opportunity to revitalize her career on the stage; and she receives better support from her friends—especially from the struggling actor Jimmy, who is more sensitive than he was in *The Gingerbread Lady*. Because Georgia is not as self-destructive as Evy, the optimistic conclusion to the movie, in which Georgia meets Polly and her ex-husband for lunch, is more plausible than the tacked-on happy ending to the play. Co-produced by Simon, *Only When I Laugh* is, in many respects, superior to the drama that inspired it.

Although *Biloxi Blues* is not the strongest play in Simon's Brighton Beach trilogy, director Mike Nichols translated it into the best film version of the three comedies (Universal, 1988). The play's free-flowing scenes—which move back and forth from a troop train, to an army barracks, to a cheap hotel, to the U.S.O.—are easily transferred to film. A significant change in the movie version is that Eugene himself—and not Arnold Epstein—becomes Sergeant Toomey's primary adversary in a final showdown with the recruits—a change that accentuates the protagonist's coming of age.

In the successful period piece *Lost in Yonkers* (Columbia, 1993) Simon extends the use of voice-overs to include Jay's narration—a technique that provides transitions between scenes and frames the story effectively. Simon also transforms Bella's mentally handicapped boyfriend, Johnny, who is not seen onstage, into an important secondary character. A minor flaw in the movie, however, is the upbeat ending, in which Bella leaves Grandma and the Yonkers apartment and heads to Florida to start a new life—a conclusion that deviates from the play's darkly comic tone.

Despite receiving four Academy Award nominations, Simon has never viewed himself as an outstanding screenwriter. Among the two dozen movie scripts that he has written (both original screenplays and adaptations of his stage comedies), he regards about seven as quality products.[4] When writing for Hollywood, Simon has always exercised less control over his material than when working on Broadway, and he admits that he misses the close collaboration between playwright and director which he normally enjoys in the theater.

Chapter 1—Understanding Neil Simon

1. Jackson R. Bryer, ed., "Neil Simon," in *The Playwright's Art: Conversations with Contemporary American Dramatists* (New Brunswick: Rutgers University Press, 1995), 232.

2. Glenn Loney, "Neil Simon," in *Contemporary Dramatists,* 4th ed., ed. D. L. Kirkpatrick (Chicago: St. James, 1988), 485.

3. Paul D. Zimmerman, "Neil Simon: Up from Success," *Newsweek,* 2 February 1970, 54.

4. Richard Meryman, "When the Funniest Writer in America Tried to be Serious," *Life,* 7 May 1971, 67.

5. Clive Barnes, "A Touching Play Tiptoes on the Heart," in *New York Theatre Critics' Reviews,* vol. 38 (1977), 110.

6. Quoted in Robert K. Johnson, *Neil Simon* (Boston: Twayne, 1983), 140.

7. Jackson R. Bryer, "An Interview with Neil Simon," *Studies in American Drama, 1945–Present* 6 (1991): 157.

8. John Lahr, "Neil Simon and Woody Allen: Images of Impotence," in *Astonish Me: Adventures in Contemporary Theater* (New York: Viking, 1973), 121–22.

9. Johnson, *Neil Simon,* 7.

10. Northrop Frye, *Anatomy of Criticism: Four Essays* (1957; reprint, New York: Atheneum, 1970), 163.

11. Bryer, "Interview," 158.

12. Daniel Walden, "Neil Simon's Jewish-style Comedies," in *From Hester Street to Hollywood: The Jewish-American Stage and Screen,* ed. Sarah Blacher Cohen (Bloomington: Indiana University Press, 1983), 152.

13. Neil Simon, *The Prisoner of Second Avenue,* in *The Collected Plays of Neil Simon,* vol. 2 (1979; reprint, New York: Plume, 1986), 253.

14. Neil Simon, *Brighton Beach Memoirs,* in *The Collected Plays of Neil Simon,* vol. 3 (New York: Random House, 1991), 485.

15. Neil Simon, *Broadway Bound,* in *Collected Plays,* vol. 3, 754, 781.

16. Quoted in Peter L. Hays, "Neil Simon and the Funny Jewish Blues," in *Neil Simon: A Casebook,* ed. Gary Konas (New York: Garland, 1997), 59–60.

17. Lawrence Linderman, "*Playboy* Interview: Neil Simon," *Playboy,* February 1979, 75.

18. Walden, "Jewish-style Comedies," 165.

19. Ibid., 156.

20. Michael Woolf, "Neil Simon," in *American Drama,* ed. Clive Bloom (New York: St. Martin's, 1995), 117.

21. T. E. Kalem, "Speak, Memory: 'Brighton Beach Memoirs,' by Neil Simon," in *New York Theatre Critics' Reviews,* vol. 44 (1983), 348.

22. Neil Simon, *Chapter Two,* in *Collected Plays,* vol. 2, 710.

23. Arvid F. Sponberg, "Men in Fancy Clothes; or, Menander on the 23rd Floor," in *A Casebook,* ed. Konas, 96.

24. Neil Simon, *The Odd Couple,* in *The Collected Plays of Neil Simon,* vol. 1 (1971; reprint, New York: Plume, 1986), 301.

25. Neil Simon, *Lost in Yonkers,* in *The Collected Plays of Neil Simon,* vol. 4 (New York: Touchstone, 1998), 153.

26. Zimmerman, "Up From Success," 55.

27. Richard Eder, "For Neil Simon, It's 'Chapter Two,'" in *New York Theatre Critics' Reviews,* vol. 38 (1977), 108.

28. Neil Simon, *Rewrites: A Memoir* (New York: Simon and Schuster, 1996), 126.

Chapter 2—*Come Blow Your Horn* and *Barefoot in the Park*

1. Simon, *Rewrites,* 50.

2. Neil Simon, *Come Blow Your Horn,* in *Collected Plays,* vol.

1, 72. Subsequent page references to this edition are given in parentheses within the text.

    3. Ellen Schiff, "Funny, He *Does* Look Jewish," in *A Casebook,* ed. Konas, 49.

    4. Edythe M. McGovern, *Neil Simon: A Critical Study* (New York: Frederick Ungar, 1979), 15.

    5. Richard Watts Jr., "A Comedy of Two Rebellious Brothers," in *New York Theatre Critics' Reviews,* vol. 22 (1961), 357.

    6. Neil Simon, "Notes from the Playwright," in McGovern, *A Critical Study,* by McGovern, 3.

    7. Neil Simon, *Barefoot in the Park,* in *Collected Plays,* vol. 1, 153. Subsequent page references to this edition are given in parentheses within the text.

    8. Johnson, *Neil Simon,* 10.

    9. McGovern, *A Critical Study,* 33.

    10. Howard Taubman, "Bubbling Comedy," in *New York Theatre Critics' Reviews,* vol. 24 (1963), 223.

    11. Norman Nadel, "'Barefoot in the Park' Due for a Long, Long Run," in *New York Theatre Critics' Reviews,* vol. 24 (1963), 222.

    12. Simon, *Rewrites,* 137.

    13. Bonamy Dobrée, "Restoration Comedy: Drama and Values," in *Comedy: Plays, Theory, and Criticism,* ed. Marvin Felheim (New York: Harcourt, Brace & World, 1962), 203.

Chapter 3—*The Odd Couple*

    1. Linderman, "*Playboy* Interview," 74.

    2. Ibid.

    3. Simon, *Rewrites,* 143.

    4. Simon, *The Odd Couple,* in *Collected Plays,* vol. 1, 248. Subsequent page references to this edition are given in parentheses within the text.

5. Ruby Cohn, "Funny Money in New York and Pendon: Neil Simon and Alan Ayckbourn," in *A Casebook,* ed. Konas, 20.

6. Robert B. Heilman, *The Ways of the World: Comedy and Society* (Seattle: University of Washington Press, 1978), 35, 37.

7. Simon, *Rewrites,* 146.

8. Paul H. Grawe, *Comedy in Space, Time, and the Imagination* (Chicago: Nelson-Hall, 1983), 41.

9. Johnson, *Neil Simon,* 22.

10. Grawe, *Comedy in Space,* 41.

11. Ibid.

12. Simon, *Rewrites,* 145.

13. Tennessee Williams, *A Streetcar Named Desire* (1947; reprint, New York: Signet, 1972), 58.

14. McGovern, *A Critical Study,* 37.

15. Howard Taubman, "Theatre: Neil Simon's 'Odd Couple,'" in *New York Theatre Critics' Reviews,* vol. 26 (1965), 364.

16. Douglas Watt, "Odd Couple Faces Eviction," in *New York Theatre Critics' Reviews,* vol. 46 (1985), 249.

17. Simon, "Notes from the Playwright," in McGovern, *A Critical Study,* 3–4.

18. Linderman, "*Playboy* Interview," 57.

Chapter 4—*Plaza Suite* and *Last of the Red Hot Lovers*

1. David Grote, *The End of Comedy: The Sitcom and the Comedic Tradition* (Hamden, Conn.: Archon, 1983), 21.

2. Richard P. Cooke, "Simon and Nichols Again," in *New York Theatre Critics' Reviews,* vol. 29 (1968), 349.

3. Neil Simon, *Plaza Suite,* in *Collected Plays,* vol. 1, 521. Subsequent page references to this edition are given in parentheses within the text.

4. Cooke, "Simon and Nichols," 349.

5. Johnson, *Neil Simon,* 37.

6. Ibid., 39.

7. Ibid.

8. Morton Gurewitch, *Comedy: The Irrational Vision* (Ithaca, N.Y.: Cornell University Press, 1975), 149–50.

9. Neil Simon, *The Play Goes On: A Memoir* (New York: Simon and Schuster, 1999), 253.

10. Simon, *Rewrites,* 301.

11. Neil Simon, *Last of the Red Hot Lovers,* in *Collected Plays,* vol. 1, 611. Subsequent page references to this edition are given in parentheses within the text.

12. Grote, *The End of Comedy,* 21.

13. Elder Olson, *The Theory of Comedy* (Bloomington: Indiana University Press, 1968), 58–59.

14. Walter Kerr, "Laughs Grow Fewer," in *New York Theatre Critics' Reviews,* vol. 31 (1970), 126.

15. Grawe, *Comedy in Space,* 26.

16. Heilman, *The Ways of the World,* 89, 50, 91–92.

Chapter 5—*The Gingerbread Lady* and *The Prisoner of Second Avenue*

1. Simon, *Rewrites,* 315.

2. Olson, *The Theory of Comedy,* 40.

3. Northrop Frye, "The Argument of Comedy," in *Comedy: Plays, Theory, and Criticism,* ed. Marvin Felheim (New York: Harcourt, Brace & World, 1962), 239.

4. Jackson R. Bryer, "An Interview with Neil Simon," in *A Casebook,* ed. Konas, 221.

5. Michael Abbott, "Neil's Women," in *A Casebook,* ed. Konas, 131.

6. Neil Simon, *The Gingerbread Lady,* in *Collected Plays,* vol. 2, 161. Subsequent page references to this edition are given in parentheses within the text.

7. McGovern, *A Critical Study,* 85.

8. Martin Gottfried, "'The Gingerbread Lady' . . . Trivial, Plotless, Characterless," in *New York Theatre Critics' Reviews,* vol. 31 (1970), 121.

9. Walter Kerr, "She Is a Woman Who Drinks, and That Is That," in *New York Theatre Critics' Reviews,* vol. 31 (1970), 119–20.

10. Johnson, *Neil Simon,* 55.

11. Stanley Kauffmann, "Last of the Red-Hot Writers," *New Republic,* 16 January 1971, 22.

12. Johnson, *Neil Simon,* 58. An account of the original ending |to the play can be found in Meryman, "When the Funniest Writer," 60D.

13. Clive Barnes, "Miss Stapleton Stars in 'Gingerbread Lady,'" in *New York Theatre Critics' Reviews,* vol. 31 (1970), 120.

14. Linderman, "*Playboy* Interview," 74.

15. Bryer, "Interview," in *Studies in American Drama,* 157.

16. Arthur Miller, *Death of a Salesman* (1949; reprint, New York: Viking Penguin, 1976), 17.

17. Simon, *The Prisoner of Second Avenue,* in *Collected Plays,* vol. 2, 237. Subsequent page references to this edition are given in parentheses within the text.

18. Olson, *The Theory of Comedy,* 51.

19. Schiff, "Funny," 49.

20. Quoted in Hays, "Funny Jewish Blues," 59.

21. Woolf, "Neil Simon," 125.

22. Simon, *Rewrites,* 341–42.

23. Ibid., 340.

24. Clive Barnes, "Stage: Creeping Paranoia and Crawling Malaise,"

New York Times, 12 November 1971, p. 55. Review of *The Prisoner of Second Avenue.*

25. Simon, *Rewrites,* 342.

26. Barnes, "Creeping Paranoia," p. 55.

Chapter 6—*The Sunshine Boys*

1. Simon, *Rewrites,* 124.

2. Simon, "Notes from the Playwright," in *A Critical Study,* by McGovern, 4.

3. Ibid., 4–5.

4. Bill Smith, *The Vaudevillians* (New York: Macmillan, 1976), 7.

5. Ibid., 10.

6. Bernard Sobel, *A Pictorial History of Vaudeville* (New York: Citadel, 1961), 87.

7. Neil Simon, *The Sunshine Boys,* in *Collected Plays,* vol. 2, 333. Subsequent page references to this edition are given in parentheses within the text.

8. McGovern, *A Critical Study,* 112.

9. Smith, *The Vaudevillians,* 250.

10. Johnson, *Neil Simon,* 64.

11. Edwin Wilson, "Another Winner for Neil Simon," in *New York Theatre Critics' Reviews,* vol. 33 (1972), 136.

12. Smith, *The Vaudevillians,* 9, 5.

13. Martin Gottfried, "Theatre: 'The Sunshine Boys,'" in *New York Theatre Critics' Reviews,* vol. 33 (1972), 135.

14. McGovern, *A Critical Study,* 120.

15. Cohn, "Funny Money," 30.

16. Zimmerman, "Up from Success," 55.

17. Simon, *Rewrites,* 360.

Chapter 7—*California Suite*

1. Sylvan Barnet et al., eds., *Types of Drama: Plays and Essays,* 5th ed. (Glenview, Ill.: Scott, Foresman, 1989), 802.

2. Quoted in Johnson, *Neil Simon,* 90.

3. Clive Barnes, "Stage: 'California Suite' Opens," in *New York Theatre Critics' Reviews,* vol. 37 (1976), 224–25.

4. Simon, *Rewrites,* 57–58.

5. McGovern, *A Critical Study,* 153.

6. Neil Simon, *California Suite,* in *Collected Plays,* vol. 2, 552. Subsequent page references to this edition are given in parentheses within the text.

7. McGovern, *A Critical Study,* 153.

8. Quoted in Norman R. Shapiro, introduction to *Four Farces by Georges Feydeau,* trans. Norman R. Shapiro (Chicago: University of Chicago Press, 1970), xxi.

9. Eric Bentley, *The Life of the Drama* (New York: Atheneum, 1967), 229.

10. Eric Bentley, "The Psychology of Farce," in *"Let's Get a Divorce" and Other Plays,* ed. Eric Bentley (New York: Hill and Wang, 1958), x.

11. Gurewitch, *Comedy,* 138.

12. Richard Grayson, "'The Fruit Brigade': Neil Simon's Gay Characters," in *A Casebook,* ed. Konas, 137.

13. Johnson, *Neil Simon,* 98.

14. Grayson, "Fruit Brigade," 137.

15. Bentley, *Life of the Drama,* 219.

16. Bentley, "Psychology," xiii.

17. Ibid., xix.

18. Linderman, *"Playboy* Interview," 74.

Chapter 8—*Chapter Two*

1. McGovern, *A Critical Study,* 171.

2. Clive Barnes, "A Touching Play Tiptoes on the Heart," in *New York Theatre Critics' Reviews,* vol. 38 (1977), 110.

3. Simon, *Chapter Two,* in *Collected Plays,* vol. 2, 699–700. Subsequent page references to this edition are given in parentheses within the text.

4. Linderman, "*Playboy* Interview," 58, 60.

5. Grawe, *Comedy in Space,* 135–36.

6. Eder, "For Neil Simon," 108.

7. Johnson, *Neil Simon,* 106–7.

8. Bryer, "Interview," *Studies in American Drama,* 167–68.

9. Walden, "Jewish-style Comedies," 163.

10. Ibid., 164.

11. J. William Worden, *Grief Counseling and Grief Therapy: A Handbook for the Mental Health Practitioner,* 2d ed. (New York: Springer, 1991), 10–18.

12. Quoted in Therese A. Rando, *Loss and Anticipatory Grief* (Lexington, Mass.: D. C. Heath, 1986), 49.

13. Neil Simon, *The Good Doctor,* in *Collected Plays,* vol. 2, 393.

Chapter 9—The Brighton Beach Trilogy

1. Kalem, "Speak, Memory," 348.

2. Simon, *Brighton Beach Memoirs,* in *Collected Plays,* vol. 3, 487. Subsequent page references to this edition are given in parentheses within the text.

3. Bryer, "Interview," *Studies in American Drama,* 175.

4. John Beaufort, "Neil Simon's Quirky, Funny New Comedy Recalls His Youth," in *New York Theatre Critics' Reviews,* vol. 44 (1983), 348–49.

5. Simon, *The Play Goes On,* 192.

6. Schiff, "Funny," 52.

7. Bryer, "Interview," *Studies in American Drama,* 168.

8. Schiff, "Funny," 52–53.

9. Frank Rich, "Stage: Neil Simon's 'Brighton Beach,'" in *New York Theatre Critics' Reviews,* vol. 44 (1983), 344.

10. Schiff, "Funny," 53.

11. Neil Simon, *Biloxi Blues,* in *Collected Plays,* vol. 3, 603. Subsequent page references to this edition are given in parentheses within the text.

12. John Beaufort, "Simon's 'Biloxi Blues' on Broadway is a Partial Success," in *New York Theatre Critics' Reviews,* vol. 46 (1985), 325.

13. William A. Henry III, "Bawdy Rites of Passage," in *New York Theatre Critics' Reviews,* vol. 46 (1985), 326.

14. Edwin Wilson, "The Funniest Play on Broadway," in *New York Theatre Critics' Reviews,* vol. 46 (1985), 324.

15. Frank Rich, "Stage: 'Biloxi Blues,' Neil Simon's New Comedy," in *New York Theatre Critics' Reviews,* vol. 46 (1985), 322.

16. Alan Cooper, "Washington Heights Doc," in *A Casebook,* ed. Konas, 46.

17. Bryer, "Interview," *Studies in American Drama,* 167–68. For further discussion of the O'Neill-Simon connection, see Glenda Frank, "Fun House Mirrors: The Neil Simon-Eugene O'Neill Dialogue," in *A Casebook,* ed. Konas, 109–25.

18. Bryer, "Interview," *Studies in American Drama,* 168.

19. Allan Wallach, "A Play That's Bound to Give Broadway a Lift," in *New York Theatre Critics' Reviews,* vol. 47 (1986), 113.

20. Simon, *Broadway Bound*, in *Collected Plays*, vol. 3, 727. Subsequent page references to this edition are given in parentheses within the text.

21. Simon, *Rewrites*, 30.

22. Ibid., 120.

23. Ibid., 29.

24. Frank Rich, "Simon's 'Broadway Bound': Coming to Terms," in *New York Theatre Critics' Reviews*, vol. 47 (1986), 112.

25. Simon, *The Play Goes On*, 202–3.

26. Rich, "Simon's 'Broadway Bound,'" 112.

27. Douglas Watt, "Well, It Has This One Terrific Scene," in *New York Theatre Critics' Reviews*, vol. 47 (1986), 114.

28. Jack Kroll, "It Only Hurts When I Laugh," in *New York Theatre Critics' Reviews*, vol. 47 (1986), 115.

29. Walter Kerr, "Seeing a Comic Mind Emerge," *New York Times*, 3 April 1983, sec. 2, pp. 3, 13.

Chapter 10—*Lost in Yonkers*

1. Bryer, "Neil Simon," in *The Playwright's Art*, 226.

2. David Richards, "The Last of the Red-Hot Playwrights," *New York Times Magazine*, 17 February 1991, 36.

3. Ibid.

4. Simon, *Lost in Yonkers*, in *Collected Plays*, vol. 4, 89. Subsequent page references to this edition are given in parentheses within the text.

5. Bette Mandl, "Beyond Laughter and Forgetting: Echoes of the Holocaust in Neil Simon's *Lost in Yonkers*," in *A Casebook*, ed. Konas, 70.

6. Mandl, "Beyond Laughter," 74.

7. Frank Rich, "Theater: Simon on Love Denied," in *New York Theatre Critics' Reviews*, vol. 52 (1991), 376.

8. William A. Henry III, "Laughter on the Brink of Tears," in *New York Theatre Critics' Reviews,* vol. 52 (1991), 381.

9. Grawe, *Comedy in Space,* 17.

10. Frye, *Anatomy,* 165.

11. Ibid., 166.

12. Ibid., 169.

13. Clive Barnes, "Lost in Yonkers, Happily Ever After," in *New York Theatre Critics' Reviews,* vol. 52 (1991), 377.

14. Quoted in Konas, *A Casebook,* 1.

15. Angela Greer, "Playwright Views Rewrites as Anything but Chore," *Independence (Kansas) Daily Register,* 18 April 1997, 2.

Chapter 11—*Jake's Women* and *Laughter on the 23rd Floor*

1. Neil Simon, *Jake's Women,* in *Collected Plays,* vol. 4, 159. Subsequent page references to this edition are given in parentheses within the text.

2. Jack Kroll, "Simon Says: Real or False," in *New York Theatre Critics' Reviews,* vol. 53 (New York: Critics' Theatre Reviews, 1992), 97.

3. Brian Rhinehart and Norman N. Holland, "*Jake's Women*: A Dialogue," in *A Casebook,* ed. Konas, 174.

4. Clive Barnes, "Everything's 'Jake': Neil Simon Gets Better With Time," in *New York Theatre Critics' Reviews,* vol. 53 (1992), 95.

5. Simon, *The Good Doctor,* in *Collected Plays,* vol. 2, 393.

6. "*Jake's Women,*" in *New York Theatre Critics' Reviews,* vol. 53 (1992), 99.

7. Otis L. Guernsey Jr., ed., "Everything You've Always Wanted to Know about . . . Neil Simon . . . but Never Had a Chance to Ask," in *Playwrights, Lyricists, Composers, on Theater* (New York: Dodd, Mead, 1964), 227.

8. Richards, "Last of the Red-Hot," 64.

9. Guernsey, "Everything You've Always Wanted," 230.

10. Richards, "Last of the Red-Hot," 32.

11. Rhinehart and Holland, "*Jake's Women*," 175.

12. Bryer, "Interview," in *A Casebook,* ed. Konas, 230.

13. Neil Simon, *Laughter on the 23rd Floor,* in *Collected Plays,* vol. 4, 280. Subsequent page references to this edition are given in parentheses within the text.

14. Jeremy Gerard, "Laughter on the 23rd Floor," in *New York Theatre Critics' Reviews,* vol. 54 (1993), 380.

15. Linda Winer, "Simon and TV Comedy," in *New York Theatre Critics' Reviews,* vol. 54 (1993), 371.

16. Frye, *Anatomy,* 163.

17. Clive Barnes, "'Laughter' Won't Floor You," in *New York Theatre Critics' Reviews,* vol. 54 (1993), 381.

18. For a discussion of riffing, see Gerald Mast, *The Comic Mind: Comedy and the Movies,* 2d ed. (Chicago: University of Chicago Press, 1979), 7.

19. Michael Feingold, "Separated at Mirth," in *New York Theatre Critics' Reviews,* vol. 54 (1993), 373.

20. In the 1953 film version of *Julius Caesar,* Marlon Brando actually played the role of Mark Antony, not Caesar.

21. Henri Bergson, "Laughter," 1900, in *Comedy,* ed. Wylie Sypher (Baltimore: Johns Hopkins University Press, 1956), 64.

22. John Lahr, "Shtick Ball," in *New York Theatre Critics' Reviews,* vol. 54 (1993), 374.

Conclusion—Between Laughter and Tears

1. From Aristotle's *Poetics* 4.7 and 5.2, quoted in Grawe, *Comedy in Space,* 3.

2. Kimball King, "General Editor's Note," in *A Casebook,* ed. Konas, vii.

3. Walter Kerr, "Simon's Funny—Don't Laugh," in *New York Theatre Critics' Reviews,* vol. 29 (1968), 347.

4. Henry, "Laughter on the Brink," 381.

Appendix—Movie Adaptations of Simon's Plays

1. Johnson, *Neil Simon,* 70, 137.

2. Quoted in Johnson, *Neil Simon,* 70–71.

3. Johnson, *Neil Simon,* 132.

4. Simon, *Rewrites,* 191.

SELECTED BIBLIOGRAPHY

Primary Works by Neil Simon

Plays

Come Blow Your Horn. New York: Samuel French, 1961. Produced 22 February 1961, Brooks Atkinson Theatre, New York.

Barefoot in the Park. New York: Random House, 1964. Produced 23 October 1963, Biltmore Theatre, New York.

The Odd Couple. New York: Random House, 1966. Produced 10 March 1965, Plymouth Theatre, New York. Revised (female) version produced 11 June 1985, Broadhurst Theatre, New York.

The Star-Spangled Girl. New York: Random House, 1967. Produced 21 December 1966, Plymouth Theatre, New York.

Plaza Suite. New York: Random House, 1969. Produced 14 February 1968, Plymouth Theatre, New York.

Last of the Red Hot Lovers. New York: Random House, 1970. Produced 28 December 1969, Eugene O'Neill Theatre, New York.

The Gingerbread Lady. New York: Random House, 1971. Produced 13 December 1970, Plymouth Theatre, New York.

The Prisoner of Second Avenue. New York: Random House, 1972. Produced 11 November 1971, Eugene O'Neill Theatre, New York.

The Sunshine Boys. New York: Random House, 1973. Produced 20 December 1972, Broadhurst Theatre, New York.

The Good Doctor. New York: Random House, 1974. Adapted from Anton Chekhov's short stories. Produced 27 November 1973, Eugene O'Neill Theatre, New York.

God's Favorite. New York: Random House, 1975. Produced 11 December 1974, Eugene O'Neill Theatre, New York.

SELECTED BIBLIOGRAPHY

California Suite. New York: Random House, 1977. Produced 30 June 1976, Eugene O'Neill Theatre, New York.

Chapter Two. New York: Random House, 1979. Produced 4 December 1977, Imperial Theatre, New York.

I Ought to Be in Pictures. New York: Random House, 1981. Produced 3 April 1980, Eugene O'Neill Theatre, New York.

Fools. New York: Random House, 1982. Produced 6 April 1981, Eugene O'Neill Theatre, New York.

Brighton Beach Memoirs. New York: Random House, 1984. Produced 27 March 1983, Alvin Theatre, New York.

Biloxi Blues. New York: Random House, 1986. Produced 28 March 1985, Neil Simon Theatre, New York.

Broadway Bound. New York: Random House, 1987. Produced 4 December 1986, Broadhurst Theatre, New York.

Rumors. New York: Random House, 1990. Produced 17 November 1988, Broadhurst Theatre, New York.

Lost in Yonkers. New York: Random House, 1991. Produced 21 February 1991, Richard Rodgers Theatre, New York.

Jake's Women. New York: Random House, 1994. Produced 24 March 1992, Neil Simon Theatre, New York.

Laughter on the 23rd Floor. New York: Random House, 1995. Produced 22 November 1993, Richard Rodgers Theatre, New York.

London Suite. New York: Samuel French, 1996. Produced 10 April 1995, Union Square Theatre, New York.

Proposals. New York: Samuel French, 1998. Produced 6 November 1997, Broadhurst Theatre, New York.

Hotel Suite. A collection of one-act plays from *Plaza Suite, California Suite,* and *London Suite.* Produced 15 June 2000, Gramercy Theatre, New York.

The Dinner Party. Produced 19 October 2000, Music Box Theatre, New York.

SELECTED BIBLIOGRAPHY

Musicals

With William Friedberg. *Adventures of Marco Polo: A Musical Fantasy.* New York: Samuel French, 1959.

With William Friedberg. *Heidi.* New York: Samuel French, 1959. Adaptation of the novel by Johanna Spyri.

Little Me. In *Collected Plays,* vol. 2, 1979, cited below. Adaptation of the novel by Patrick Dennis. Produced 17 November 1962, Lunt-Fontanne Theatre, New York.

Sweet Charity. New York: Random House, 1966. Based on Federico Fellini's screenplay *Nights of Cabiria.* Produced 29 January 1966, Palace Theatre, New York.

Promises, Promises. New York: Random House, 1969. Based on the screenplay *The Apartment* by Billy Wilder and I. A. L. Diamond. Produced 1 December 1968, Shubert Theatre, New York.

They're Playing Our Song. New York: Random House, 1980. Produced 11 February 1979, Imperial Theatre, New York.

The Goodbye Girl. Unpublished libretto. Adaptation of Simon's 1977 screenplay, cited below. Produced 4 March 1993, Marquis Theatre, New York.

Screenplays

After the Fox. Original screenplay. United Artists, 1966.

Barefoot in the Park. Simon's adaptation of his play. Paramount, 1967.

The Odd Couple. Simon's adaptation of his play. Paramount, 1968.

The Out-of-Towners. Original screenplay. Paramount, 1970.

Plaza Suite. Simon's adaptation of his play. Paramount, 1971.

The Heartbreak Kid. Adaptation of Bruce Jay Friedman's short story. Twentieth Century Fox, 1972.

SELECTED BIBLIOGRAPHY

Last of the Red Hot Lovers. Simon's adaptation of his play. Paramount, 1972.

The Sunshine Boys. Simon's adaptation of his play. MGM, 1975.

The Prisoner of Second Avenue. Simon's adaptation of his play. Warner Brothers, 1975.

Murder By Death. Original screenplay. Columbia, 1976.

The Goodbye Girl. Original screenplay. Warner Brothers, 1977.

The Cheap Detective. Original screenplay. Columbia, 1978.

California Suite. Simon's adaptation of his play. Columbia, 1978.

Chapter Two. Simon's adaptation of his play. Columbia, 1979.

Seems Like Old Times. Original screenplay. Columbia, 1980.

Only When I Laugh. Simon's adaptation of his play *The Gingerbread Lady.* Columbia, 1981.

I Ought to Be in Pictures. Simon's adaptation of his play. Twentieth Century Fox, 1982.

Max Dugan Returns. Original screenplay. Twentieth Century Fox, 1983.

The Slugger's Wife. Original screenplay. Columbia, 1985.

Brighton Beach Memoirs. Simon's adaptation of his play. Universal, 1986.

Biloxi Blues. Simon's adaptation of his play. Universal, 1988.

The Marrying Man. Original screenplay. Hollywood Pictures, 1991.

Lost in Yonkers. Simon's adaptation of his play. Columbia, 1993.

The Odd Couple II. Original screenplay. Paramount, 1998.

Collections

The Collected Plays of Neil Simon. Vol. 1. New York: Plume, 1986. Includes *Come Blow Your Horn, Barefoot in the Park, The Odd Couple, The Star-Spangled Girl, Plaza Suite, Promises, Promises, Last of the Red Hot Lovers.* Originally published as *The Comedy of Neil Simon* (New York: Random House, 1971).

SELECTED BIBLIOGRAPHY

The Collected Plays of Neil Simon. Vol. 2. 1979. Reprint, New York: Plume, 1986. Includes *The Sunshine Boys, Little Me, The Gingerbread Lady, The Prisoner of Second Avenue, The Good Doctor, God's Favorite, California Suite, Chapter Two.*

The Collected Plays of Neil Simon. Vol. 3. New York: Random House, 1991. Includes *Sweet Charity, They're Playing Our Song, I Ought to Be in Pictures, Fools, The Odd Couple* (female version), *Brighton Beach Memoirs, Biloxi Blues, Broadway Bound.*

The Collected Plays of Neil Simon. Vol. 4. New York: Touchstone, 1998. Includes *Rumors, Lost in Yonkers, Jake's Women, Laughter on the 23rd Floor, London Suite.*

Autobiography

Rewrites: A Memoir. New York: Simon and Schuster, 1996.
The Play Goes On: A Memoir. New York: Simon and Schuster, 1999.

Secondary Works

Bibliography

King, Kimball. *Ten Modern American Playwrights: An Annotated Bibliography,* 215–33. New York: Garland, 1982.

Morrow, Laura. "Neil Simon." In *American Playwrights since 1945: A Guide to Scholarship, Criticism, and Performance.* Edited by Philip C. Kolin, 420–36. Westport, Conn.: Greenwood, 1989.

Interviews

Bryer, Jackson R. "An Interview with Neil Simon." In *Neil Simon: A Casebook,* edited by Gary Konas, 217–32. New York: Garland, 1997.

SELECTED BIBLIOGRAPHY

———. "An Interview with Neil Simon." *Studies in American Drama: 1945–Present* 6 (1991): 153–76.

———, ed. "Neil Simon." In *The Playwright's Art: Conversations with Contemporary American Dramatists,* 221–40. New Brunswick: Rutgers University Press, 1995.

Guernsey, Otis L. Jr., ed. "Everything You've Always Wanted to Know about . . . Neil Simon . . . but Never Had a Chance to Ask." In *Playwrights, Lyricists, Composers, on Theater,* 227–42. New York: Dodd, Mead, 1964.

Linderman, Lawrence. "*Playboy* Interview: Neil Simon." *Playboy,* February 1979.

Books

Johnson, Robert K. *Neil Simon.* Boston: Twayne, 1983. Intelligent survey of Simon's work up until the early 1980s; includes discussions of Simon's musicals and screenplays.

Konas, Gary, ed. *Neil Simon: A Casebook.* New York: Garland, 1997. Outstanding collection of contemporary critical views on Simon.

McGovern, Edythe M. *Neil Simon: A Critical Study.* New York: Frederick Ungar, 1979. Early study of Simon that relies heavily on plot summaries but contains valuable insights.

Rando, Therese A. *Loss and Anticipatory Grief.* Lexington, Mass.: D. C. Heath, 1986.

Shapiro, Norman R., trans. *Four Farces by Georges Feydeau.* Chicago: University of Chicago Press, 1970.

Worden, J. William. *Grief Counseling and Grief Therapy: A Handbook for the Mental Health Practitioner.* 2d ed. New York: Springer, 1991.

SELECTED BIBLIOGRAPHY

Articles and Chapters in Books

Greer, Angela. "Playwright Views Rewrites as Anything But Chore." *Independence (Kans.) Daily Register,* 18 April 1997.

Lahr, John. "Neil Simon and Woody Allen: Images of Impotence." In *Astonish Me: Adventures in Contemporary Theater,* 120–36. New York: Viking, 1973.

Loney, Glenn. "Neil Simon." In *Contemporary Dramatists.* 4th ed., edited by D. L. Kirkpatrick, 484–86. Chicago: St. James, 1988.

Meryman, Richard. "When the Funniest Writer in America Tried to Be Serious." *Life,* 7 May 1971.

Richards, David. "The Last of the Red-Hot Playwrights." *New York Times Magazine* (17 February 1991): 30–32, 36, 57, 64.

Walden, Daniel. "Neil Simon's Jewish-style Comedies." In *From Hester Street to Hollywood: The Jewish-American Stage and Screen,* edited by Sarah Blacher Cohen, 152–66. Bloomington: Indiana University Press, 1983.

Woolf, Michael. "Neil Simon." In *American Drama,* edited by Clive Bloom, 117–30. New York: St. Martin's, 1995.

Zimmerman, Paul D. "Neil Simon: Up from Success." *Newsweek,* 2 February 1970, 52–56.

Reviews

Barnes, Clive. "Everything's 'Jake': Neil Simon Gets Better with Time." In *New York Theatre Critics' Reviews,* vol. 53, 95. New York: Critics' Theatre Reviews, 1992. First published in *New York Post,* 25 March 1992. Review of *Jake's Women*

———. "'Laughter' Won't Floor You." In *New York Theatre Critics' Reviews,* vol. 54, 381. New York: Critics' Theatre Reviews, 1993. First published in *New York Post,* 23 November 1993. Review of *Laughter on the 23rd Floor.*

SELECTED BIBLIOGRAPHY

———. "Lost in Yonkers, Happily Ever After." In *New York Theatre Critics' Reviews,* vol. 52, 377. New York: Critics' Theatre Reviews, 1991. First published in *New York Post,* 22 February 1991.

———. "Miss Stapleton Stars in 'Gingerbread Lady.'" In *New York Theatre Critics' Reviews,* vol. 31, 120. New York: Critics' Theatre Reviews, 1970. First published in *New York Times* 14 December 1970.

———. "Stage: Creeping Paranoia and Crawling Malaise." *New York Times,* 12 November 1971. Review of *The Prisoner of Second Avenue.*

———. "Stage: 'California Suite' Opens." In *New York Theatre Critics' Reviews,* vol. 37, 224–25. New York: Critics' Theatre Reviews, 1976. First published in *New York Times,* 11 June 1976.

———. "A Touching Play Tiptoes on the Heart." In *New York Theatre Critics' Reviews,* vol. 38, 110. New York: Critics' Theatre Reviews, 1977. First published in *New York Post,* 5 December 1977. Review of *Chapter Two.*

Beaufort, John. "Neil Simon's Quirky, Funny New Comedy Recalls His Youth." In *New York Theatre Critics' Reviews,* vol. 44, 348–49. New York: Critics' Theatre Reviews, 1983. First published in *Christian Science Monitor,* 30 March 1983. Review of *Brighton Beach Memoirs.*

———. "Simon's 'Biloxi Blues' on Broadway Is a Partial Success." In *New York Theatre Critics' Reviews,* vol. 46, 325–26. New York: Critics' Theatre Reviews, 1985. First published in *Christian Science Monitor,* 29 March 1985.

Cooke, Richard P. "Simon and Nichols Again." In *New York Theatre Critics' Reviews,* vol. 29, 349–50. New York: Critics' Theatre Reviews, 1968. First published in *Wall Street Journal,* 16 February 1968. Review of *Plaza Suite.*

Eder, Richard. "For Neil Simon, It's 'Chapter Two.'" In *New York Theatre Critics' Reviews,* vol. 38, 108. New York: Critics' Theatre

SELECTED BIBLIOGRAPHY

Reviews, 1977. First published in *New York Times,* 5 December 1977.

Feingold, Michael. "Separated at Mirth." In *New York Theatre Critics' Reviews,* vol. 54, 373. New York: Critics' Theatre Reviews, 1993. First published in *Village Voice,* 30 November 1993. Review of *Laughter on the 23rd Floor.*

Gerard, Jeremy. "Laughter on the 23rd Floor." In *New York Theatre Critics' Reviews,* vol. 54, 380. New York: Critics' Theatre Reviews, 1993. First published in *Variety,* 6 December 1993.

Gottfried, Martin. "'The Gingerbread Lady' . . . Trivial, Plotless, Characterless." In *New York Theatre Critics' Reviews,* vol. 31, 121–22. New York: Critics' Theatre Reviews, 1970. First published in *Women's Wear Daily,* 15 December 1970.

———. "Theatre: 'The Sunshine Boys.'" In *New York Theatre Critics' Reviews,* vol. 33, 135. New York: Critics' Theatre Reviews, 1972. First published in *Women's Wear Daily,* 22 December 1972.

Henry, William A. III. "Laughter on the Brink of Tears." In *New York Theatre Critics' Reviews,* vol. 52, 381. New York: Critics' Theatre Reviews, 1991. First published in *Time,* 4 March 1991. Review of *Lost in Yonkers.*

———. "Bawdy Rites of Passage." In *New York Theatre Critics' Reviews,* vol. 46, 326–27. New York: Critics' Theatre Reviews, 1985. First published in *Time,* 8 April 1985. Review of *Biloxi Blues.*

"Jake's Women." In *New York Theatre Critics' Reviews,* vol. 53, 99. New York: Critics' Theatre Reviews, 1992. First published in *Time,* 30 March 1992.

Kalem, T. E. "Speak, Memory: 'Brighton Beach Memoirs,' by Neil Simon." In *New York Theatre Critics' Reviews,* vol. 44, 347–48. New York: Critics' Theatre Reviews, 1983. First published in *Time,* 11 April 1983.

Kauffmann, Stanley. "Last of the Red-Hot Writers." *New Republic,* 16 January 1971. Review of *The Gingerbread Lady.*

SELECTED BIBLIOGRAPHY

Kerr, Walter. "Laughs Grow Fewer." In *New York Theatre Critics' Reviews,* vol. 31, 126. New York: Critics' Theatre Reviews, 1970. First published in *New York Times,* 4 January 1970. Review of *Last of the Red Hot Lovers.*

———. "Seeing a Comic Mind Emerge." *New York Times,* 3 April 1983. Review of *Brighton Beach Memoirs.*

———. "She Is a Woman Who Drinks, and That Is That." In *New York Theatre Critics' Reviews,* vol. 31, 119–20. New York: Critics' Theatre Reviews, 1970. First published in *New York Times,* 20 December 1970. Review of *The Gingerbread Lady.*

———. "Simon's Funny—Don't Laugh." In *New York Theatre Critics' Reviews,* vol. 29, 347. New York: Critics' Theatre Reviews, 1968. First published in *New York Times,* 25 February 1968. Review of *Plaza Suite.*

Kroll, Jack. "It Only Hurts When I Laugh." In *New York Theatre Critics' Reviews,* vol. 47, 115. New York: Critics' Theatre Reviews, 1986. First published in *Newsweek,* 15 December 1986. Review of *Broadway Bound.*

———. "Simon Says: Real or False." In *New York Theatre Critics' Reviews,* vol. 53, 97. New York: Critics' Theatre Reviews, 1992. First published in *Newsweek,* 6 April 1992. Review of *Jake's Women.*

Lahr, John. "Shtick Ball." In *New York Theatre Critics' Reviews,* vol. 54, 374–75. New York: Critics' Theatre Reviews, 1993. First published in *New Yorker,* 20 December 1993. Review of *Laughter on the 23rd Floor.*

Nadel, Norman. "'Barefoot in the Park' Due for a Long, Long Run." In *New York Theatre Critics' Reviews,* vol. 24, 222. New York: Critics' Theatre Reviews, 1963. First published in *New York World-Telegram and The Sun,* 24 October 1963.

Rich, Frank. "Simon's 'Broadway Bound': Coming to Terms." In *New York Theatre Critics' Reviews,* vol. 47, 112–13. New York: Critics'

SELECTED BIBLIOGRAPHY

Theatre Reviews, 1986. First published in *New York Times,* 5 December 1986.

———. "Stage: 'Biloxi Blues,' Neil Simon's New Comedy." In *New York Theatre Critics' Reviews,* vol. 46, 322. New York: Critics' Theatre Reviews, 1985. First published in *New York Times,* 29 March 1985.

———. "Stage: Neil Simon's 'Brighton Beach.'" In *New York Theatre Critics' Reviews,* vol. 44, 344. New York: Critics' Theatre Reviews, 1983. First published in *New York Times,* 28 March 1983.

———. "Theater: Simon on Love Denied." In *New York Theatre Critics' Reviews,* vol. 52, 376. New York: Critics' Theatre Reviews, 1991. First published in *New York Times,* 22 February 1991. Review of *Lost in Yonkers.*

Taubman, Howard. "Bubbling Comedy." In *New York Theatre Critics' Reviews,* vol. 24, 223. New York: Critics' Theatre Reviews, 1963. First published in *New York Times,* 24 October 1963. Review of *Barefoot in the Park.*

———. "Theatre: Neil Simon's 'Odd Couple.'" In *New York Theatre Critics' Reviews,* vol. 26, 363–64. New York: Critics' Theatre Reviews, 1965. First published in *New York Times,* 11 March 1965.

Wallach, Allan. "A Play That's Bound to Give Broadway a Lift." In *New York Theatre Critics' Reviews,* vol. 47, 113. New York: Critics' Theatre Reviews, 1986. First published in *New York Newsday,* 5 December 1986. Review of *Broadway Bound.*

Watt, Douglas. "Odd Couple Faces Eviction." In *New York Theatre Critics' Reviews,* vol. 46, 249–50. New York: Critics' Theatre Reviews, 1985. First published in *New York Daily News,* 12 June 1985.

———. "Well, It Has This One Terrific Scene." In *New York Theatre Critics' Reviews,* vol. 47, 114. New York: Critics' Theatre Reviews,

1986. First published in *New York Daily News,* 12 December 1986. Review of *Broadway Bound.*

Watts, Richard Jr. "A Comedy of Two Rebellious Brothers." In *New York Theatre Critics' Reviews,* vol. 22, 357. New York: Critics' Theatre Reviews, 1961. First published in *New York Post,* 23 February 1961. Review of *Come Blow Your Horn.*

Wilson, Edwin. "Another Winner for Neil Simon." In *New York Theatre Critics' Reviews,* vol. 33, 136. New York: Critics' Theatre Reviews, 1972. First published in *Wall Street Journal,* 22 December 1972. Review of *The Sunshine Boys.*

————. "The Funniest Play on Broadway." In *New York Theatre Critics' Reviews,* vol. 46, 324–25. New York: Critics' Theatre Reviews, 1985. First published in *Wall Street Journal,* 2 April 1985. Review of *Biloxi Blues.*

Winer, Linda. "Simon and TV Comedy." In *New York Theatre Critics' Reviews,* vol. 54, 371. New York: Critics' Theatre Reviews, 1993. First published in *New York Newsday,* 23 November 1993. Review of *Laughter on the 23rd Floor.*

Comedy: General Sources

Bentley, Eric. *The Life of the Drama.* New York: Atheneum, 1967.

————. "The Psychology of Farce." In *"Let's Get a Divorce" and Other Plays,* edited by Eric Bentley, vii-xx. New York: Hill and Wang, 1958.

Bergson, Henri. "Laughter." 1900. In *Comedy,* edited by Wylie Sypher, 61–190. Baltimore: Johns Hopkins University Press, 1956.

Felheim, Marvin, ed. *Comedy: Plays, Theory, and Criticism.* New York: Harcourt, Brace & World, 1962.

Frye, Northrop. *An Anatomy of Criticism: Four Essays.* 1957. Reprint, New York: Atheneum, 1970.

SELECTED BIBLIOGRAPHY

Grawe, Paul H. *Comedy in Space, Time, and the Imagination.* Chicago: Nelson-Hall, 1983.

Grote, David. *The End of Comedy: The Sitcom and the Comedic Tradition.* Hamden, Conn.: Archon, 1983.

Gurewitch, Morton L. *Comedy: The Irrational Vision.* Ithaca: Cornell University Press, 1975.

Heilman, Robert B. *The Ways of the World: Comedy and Society.* Seattle: University of Washington Press, 1978.

Mast, Gerald. *The Comic Mind: Comedy and the Movies.* 2 ed. Chicago: University of Chicago Press, 1979.

Olson, Elder. *The Theory of Comedy.* Bloomington: Indiana University Press, 1968.

Smith, Bill. *The Vaudevillians.* New York: Macmillan, 1976.

Sobel, Bernard. *A Pictorial History of Vaudeville.* New York: Citadel, 1961.

INDEX

INDEX

INDEX